PLAY IT SAFE!

Please respect all trail users — walkers, runners, photographers, bikers and those using mobility aides. The trails are for everyone to enjoy! Obey all traffic signs, and please pull off to the side when observing flora, fauna and scenic views. Please adhere to trail restrictions and hours. (If night riding is allowed, reflective clothing is recommended.) Always wear necessary helmets and travel with a buddy in case of emergencies. And please — camp in campgrounds only. Mutual respect for the land, adjoining landowners and other trail users will make everyone's experience much more enjoyable!

CAUTION: Hunting is allowed on some of the trails and is prohibited on others. Also, snowmobiling, cross-country skiing, and equestrian use may be restricted to certain areas or conditions. If you have any questions or concerns, check with the information sources listed for each trail.

TRAIL PASSES

Several trails require a pass, which can be purchased for a small fee. This helps the county or city maintain the trail for your enjoyment. Thank you for purchasing your pass!

HANDICAP-ACCESSIBILITY

Cement, asphalt, and crushed limestone trails with low grades have been identified as handicap-accessible by the use of a handicap-accessible symbol at the top of the map. Trails with steeper grades or alternative surfaces *may* be suitable for individuals with wheelchairs or walking aids, but this decision is best made on an individual basis. For this reason handicap-accessible facilities such as restrooms and parking lots have also been noted for trails that are not considered handicap-accessible. These features are denoted with an asterisk under the trailhead amenities section.

As you discover corrections needed for future editions of this guide, please send them to the Iowa Natural Heritage Foundation office. Your help will make the next edition even better!

- - - Proposed
- H Hospital
- PASS Trail pass required
- Handicap-accessible
- Iowa Natural Heritage Foundation project

TABLE OF CONTENTS

1 - Bill Riley Bike Trail
2 - Cedar River Greenbelt Trail & Harry Cook Nature Trail
3 - Cedar Valley Lakes Trail Network
4 - Cedar Valley Nature Trail
5 - Chichaqua Valley Trail
6 - Cinder Path
7 - Clive Greenbelt Trail
8 - Comet Trail
9 - Dickinson County Spine Trail
10 - Duck Creek Parkway Trail & Riverfront Trail
11 - East River Bike Trail
12 - Fort Dodge Nature Trail
13 - Franklin Grove Heritage Trail
14 - Great River Road Trail
15 - Great Western Trail
16 - Heart of Iowa Nature Trail
17 - Heritage Trail
18 - Hoover Nature Trail
19 - Jackson County Recreation Trail
20 - Kewash Nature Trail
21 - Linn Creek Greenbelt Parkway
22 - Orange City/Alton Puddle Jumper Trail
23 - Pioneer Trail
24 - Prairie Farmer Recreational Trail
25 - Raccoon River Valley Trail
26 - River City Greenbelt and Trail System
27 - Sac and Fox Trail
28 - Sauk Rail Trail
29 - Saylorville-Des Moines River Trail
30 - Shell Rock River Trail
31 - Spencer Recreational Trail
32 - Storm Lake LakeTrail
33 - Three Rivers Trail
34 - Volksweg Trail
35 - Wabash Trace Nature Trail
36 - Wapsi-Great Western Line

ENJOY IOWA'S RECREATION TRAILS!

© 1994 by Iowa Natural Heritage Foundation. Second Edition.

Major support for this guide provided by:
- Blue Cross and Blue Shield of Iowa
- Brenton Bank
- Iowa Department of Transportation

Production assistance by Amy Kern, R. J. McElroy Communications Intern for the Iowa Natural Heritage Foundation, and Chichaqua Bend Studios, Ames, Iowa.

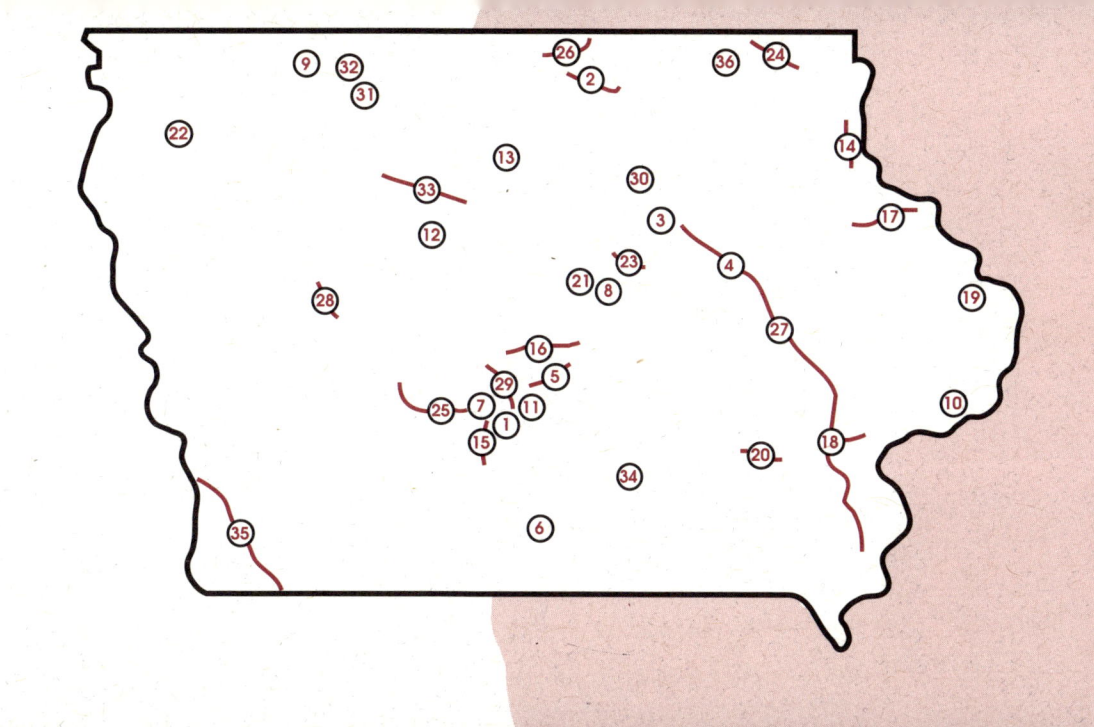

BRENTON *Bank*

Member FDIC

We're Trail Blazers in the World of Finance.

CASEY'S GENERAL STORE

HOMEMADE DONUTS To Go

HOMEMADE PIZZA To Go

Casey's Coffee Club
Refills Only 10¢

A Convenience Store and A Whole Lot More!

WELCOME TO IOWA'S TRAILS!

Matt Phalen

BILL RILEY BIKE TRAIL 1

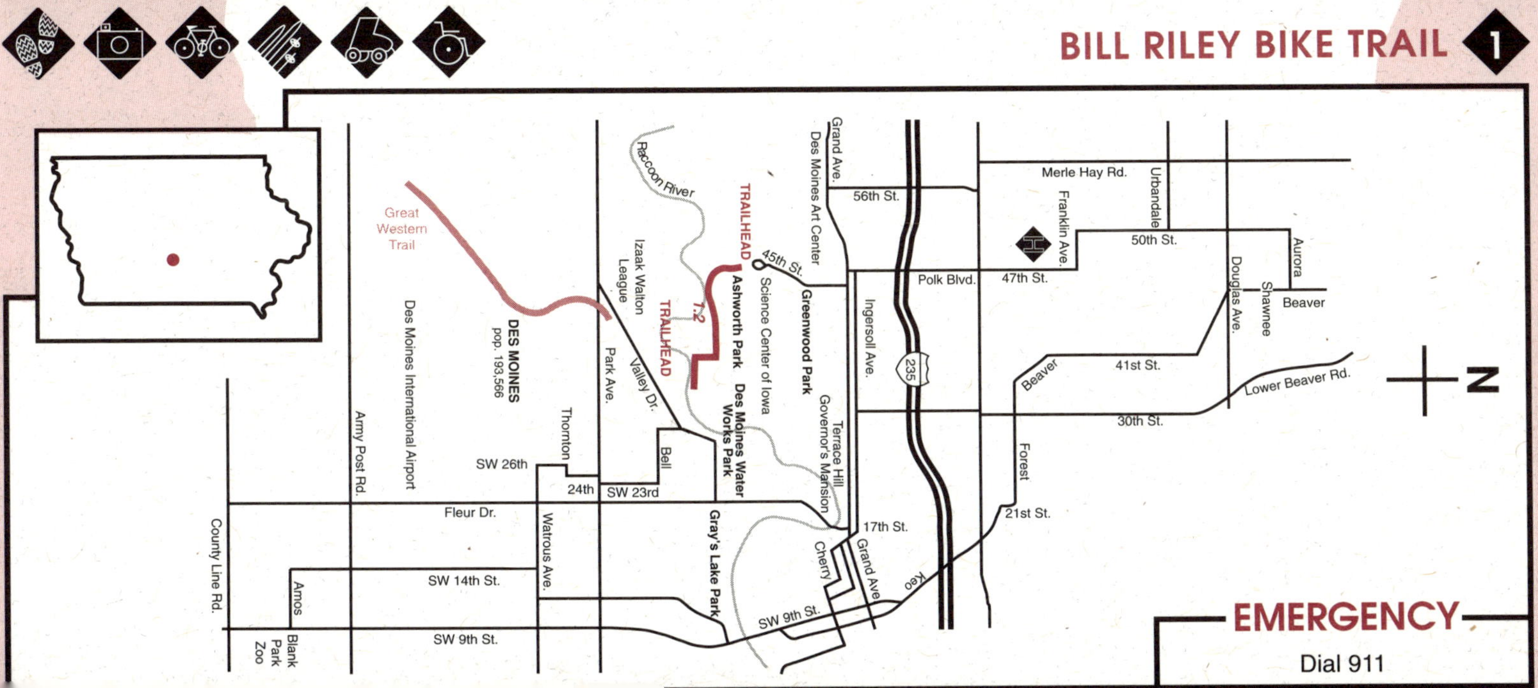

BILL RILEY BIKE TRAIL - Des Moines

This trail is named for longtime civic leader and businessman, Bill Riley. Riley, an outdoor enthusiast and television personality, organized local fund raising efforts in Des Moines in the early 1970s to finance this trail, the first in the Capital City metro area. Many people use connecting park roads as trails, increasing the length from 1.2 miles to 5 miles.

The trail offers outstanding scenery as it winds its way through Ashworth Park and along the Raccoon River. The flatness of the trail makes it a popular route for families who share an interest in exercise and fun. It connects a major city park with various foot paths and roads in Des Moines Water Works Park. Access to the Great Western Trail is planned.

The Des Moines metro area offers much to see and explore. The Water Works Park and Arboretum has 1500 trees and 300 varieties of flowering crabapple trees that usually bloom in May. The Des Moines Art Center, in Greenwood Park, houses a collection of 19th and 20th century art and sponsors exhibits and educational programs throughout the year. The Science Center of Iowa is nearby in Ashworth Park.

Terrace Hill, designated as the Governor's mansion in 1972, is a fine example of a Victorian home. Tours are available.

Among the many festivals and events in Des Moines that trail users may enjoy are the Drake Relays and Festival held in April and the Garden Fair at the Botanical Center. In August, the exciting Iowa State Fair takes place, followed by the Sherman Hill Walking Tour in September, where visitors can view homes built from 1885 to 1905. Information on other events may be obtained from the Des Moines Convention & Visitors Bureau, 601 Locust Ave., Des Moines, Iowa 50309; (515) 286-4960.

DES MOINES

North trailhead at Ashworth Pool parking lot on 45th Street: parking*, restrooms, picnic tables, phones, drinking water
South trailhead at Water Works Park, 2200 Valley Drive: parking*, picnic tables
City facilities
Bed & breakfasts
Bike shop/repair/ rental
Boat rental
City parks
Groceries
Hospitals
Hotels/motels
Restaurants

*Handicap-accessible

HOURS: Open year-round, 6:00 a.m.-10:00 p.m., except when snow or ice conditions exist.
FEE: No user fee required.
TRAIL FACTS: Total miles: 1.2; **Surfacing:** Asphalt
INFORMATION: City of Des Moines Park & Recreation Dept., 3226 University, Des Moines, Iowa 50311; (515) 237-1386

CEDAR RIVER GREENBELT & HARRY COOK NATURE TRAILS

EMERGENCY
Dial 911
Mitchell County Sheriff: (515) 732-4740

TRAILHEAD

Spring Park Rd.
Rest Area and Scenic Vista
Falk's Wildlife Area
River Road
Interstate Park
Mitchell Dam and Powerhouse
Cedar River
Sugar Creek
Mitchell County Historical Museum

OSAGE pop. 3,718
MITCHELL pop. 193

T42 · T38 · 34 · 6 · 218 · A45 · T28 · 193

N

CEDAR RIVER GREENBELT TRAIL & HARRY COOK NATURE TRAIL - Mitchell County

Trail users may want to take their fishing poles with them on the Cedar River Greenbelt Trail! Not only is this trail known for its wooded, rolling scenery, but the river is noted for its abundance of walleye, channel catfish and small-mouth bass. The four-mile recreation trail parallels the west side of the Cedar River from Interstate Park, in Mitchell, to Falk's Wildlife Area, two miles west of Osage. Fishing from the riverbank near the trail is allowed.

A gap of one-half mile separates the Cedar River trail from the Harry Cook Nature Trail. Trail users need to cross the Highway 9 bridge and travel a short distance on Spring Park Road before reaching Spring Park, the eastern trailhead for the Harry Cook trail. From the park the trail winds along Cedar River and Sugar Creek before ending in Osage. The two-mile trail features prairie and woodlands containing native species. Examples of wildlife seen along the trail include fox, turkey, beaver, mink, and blue herons.

For tourism information, contact the Osage Chamber of Commerce, 618 Main Street, Osage, Iowa 50461, (515) 732-3163; or the Mitchell County Conservation Board listed below.

Ty Smedes

MITCHELL
Trailhead at southwest end of Cedar River Bridge at Mitchell, near Interstate Park: parking*, picnic tables, (restrooms*, drinking water, shelter and camping available at Interstate Park)
Trailhead at T-28 entrance, 1.5 miles south of Mitchell: parking
City facilities
County park
Restaurants

OSAGE
Trailhead at Falk's Wildlife Area, off Highway 9: parking, equestrian parking
Trailhead at Highway 9 entrance, 1 mile west of Osage: parking
Trailhead at Spring Park: parking*, picnic tables, shelter
Trailhead at 1st Street South: parking
City facilities
Bike repair
Camping
City park
Groceries
Hospital
Lodging
Restaurants

*Handicap-accessible

HOURS: Open year-round, no restrictive hours. **FEE:** No user fee required.
TRAIL FACTS: Total miles: Cedar River Greenbelt Trail: 4; Harry Cook Nature Trail: 2; **Surfacing:** Crushed limestone; **Restrictions**: Hunting and equestrian use are only allowed on the Cedar River Greenbelt Trail. (Hunting is restricted to publicly-owned sections of the Cedar River Greenbelt Trail.)
INFORMATION: Mitchell County Conservation Board, 415 Lime Kiln Road, Osage, Iowa 50461, (515) 732-5204 or Osage Parks and Recreation, 114 South 7th, Osage, Iowa 50461, (515) 732-4674

CEDAR VALLEY LAKES TRAIL NETWORK

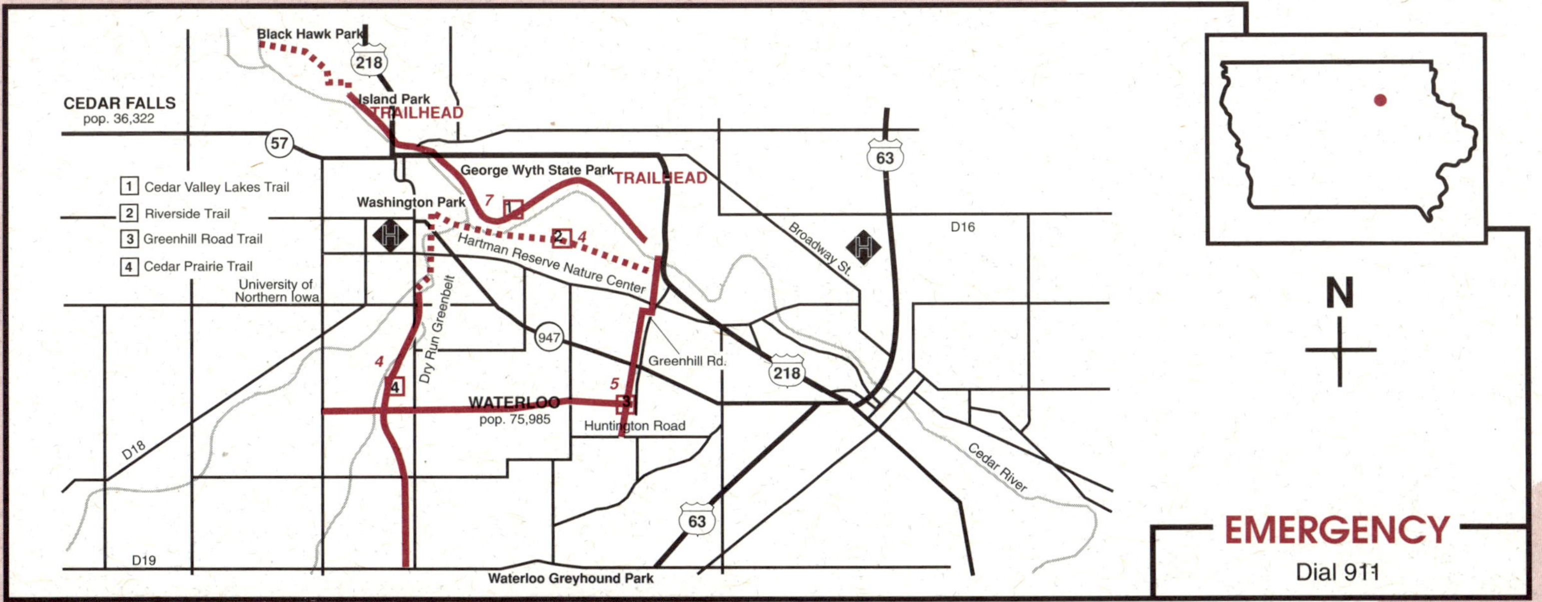

EMERGENCY
Dial 911

1	Cedar Valley Lakes Trail
2	Riverside Trail
3	Greenhill Road Trail
4	Cedar Prairie Trail

WATERLOO pop. 75,985

CEDAR FALLS pop. 36,322

CEDAR VALLEY LAKES TRAIL NETWORK - Black Hawk County

The Cedar Valley Lakes Trail Network is an intricate recreational system uniting the park and recreation facilities of Cedar Falls and Waterloo. Currently, the Cedar Valley Lakes Project is in the process of building two new lakes, expanding two existing lakes, and incorporating the trails into each lake recreational area.

1. CEDAR VALLEY LAKES TRAIL
Total miles: App. 7; **Completed segments:** 5 miles starting at George Wyth and ending at Island Park; **Completion date:** Late 1994; **Trail access:** Island Park and George Wyth Park. (Both park trailheads offer parking*, restrooms*, phones, drinking water and picnic tables; George Wyth Park includes camping, swimming and boat access.) The Cedar Valley Lakes Trail extends through George Wyth State Park, Cedar Falls' central business district, urban areas, undeveloped woodlands, wooded pastures and grasslands.

2. RIVERSIDE TRAIL
Total miles: App. 2.5; **Completion date:** 1994 (The old railway is open for interim use - hiking, cross-country skiing only); **Trail access:** Cedar Prairie Trail, Hartman Reserve, Greenhill Road Trail. This trail offers high blufflands with an overview of Cedar Valley Lakes, plus low woodlands and forest.

3. GREENHILL ROAD TRAIL
Total miles: App. 5; **Completed segments:** Greenhill Road/218 So. to Huntington Road; and west to Hudson Road. **Trail access:** Greenhill Road. Greenhill Road Trail runs through urban areas and crosses the Cedar River.

4. CEDAR PRAIRIE TRAIL
Total miles: App. 4; **Completed segments:** 3 miles Ridgeway to University Ave.; **Completion date:** 1993-1994. Agricultural and urban areas will be visited by this trail.

CEDAR FALLS/WATERLOO
City facilities
Bed & breakfasts
Bike shops/repair/rental
Camping
City parks
Groceries
Hospital
Hotels/motels
Information center
Nature center
Restaurants

*Handicap-accessible

Many recreational and cultural opportunities are offered by the Cedar Falls/Waterloo metropolitan area. For visitor information contact the Waterloo Convention & Visitors Bureau, 215 E. Fourth St., Waterloo, Iowa 50704; (319) 233-8350. Or contact Cedar Falls Chamber of Commerce, 10 Main St., Cedar Falls, Iowa 50613; (319) 266-3593.

HOURS: Open year-round; no restrictive hours, except within George Wyth State Park, which is open 4:00 a.m.-10:30 p.m.
FEE: No user fee required.
TRAIL FACTS: Total mileage of trail system: 20; Miles completed: 13; Surfacing: Asphalt
INFORMATION: Black Hawk County Conservation Board, 2410 W. Lone Tree Road, Cedar Falls, Iowa 50613; (319) 266-6813 or George Wyth State Park, 3659 Wyth Road, Waterloo, Iowa 50703; (319) 232-5505

CEDAR VALLEY NATURE TRAIL 4

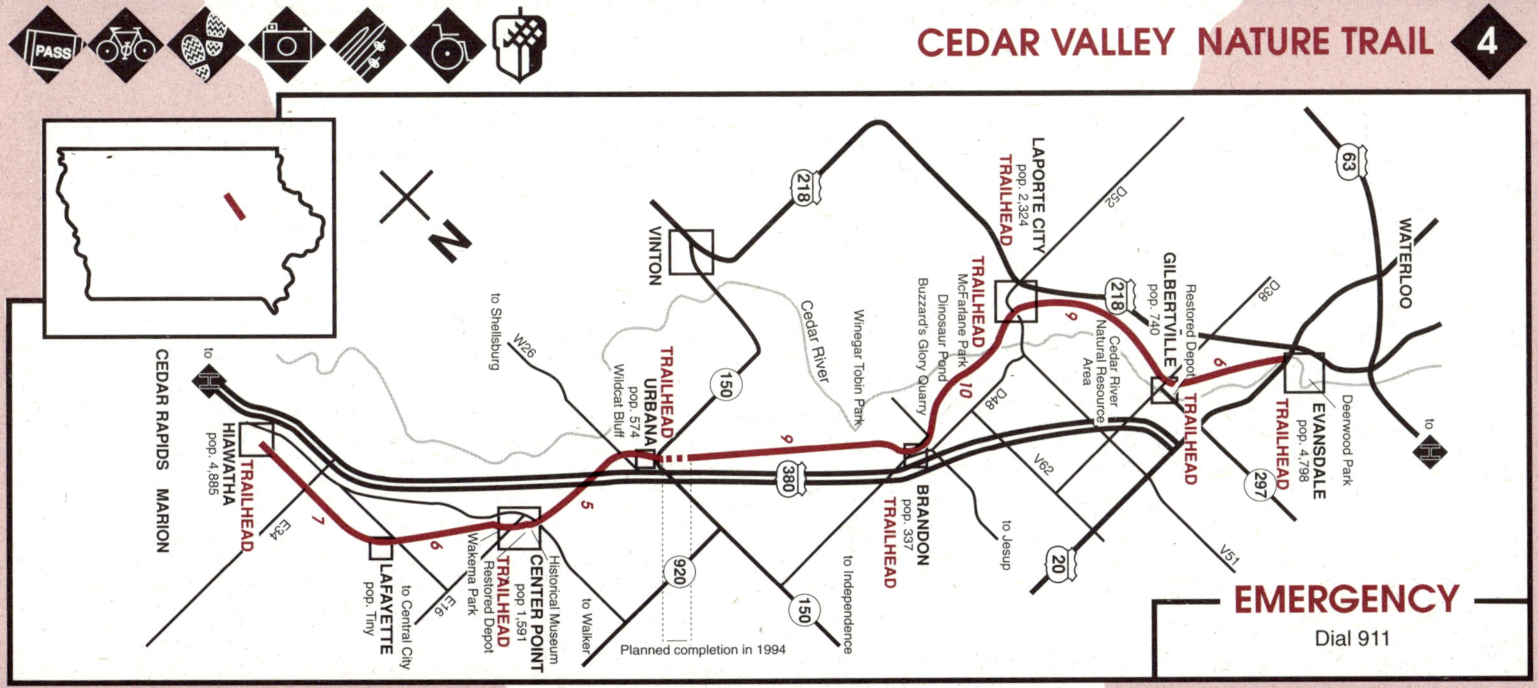

CEDAR VALLEY NATURE TRAIL
- Black Hawk, Buchanan, Benton and Linn Counties

This linear park follows a route through the Cedar River bottomlands, along forested banks of the river and across fields where stands of trees are punctuated by open vistas. Occasional stream valleys and small rural towns break up the route. It is an excellent place to observe deer, woodchucks, wild turkey, songbirds and wildflowers. Historical landmarks, archaeological sites and two restored railroad depots also add an interest to the trail.

Throughout the summer visitors can enjoy outdoor activities located on or near the trail. Every second Saturday from June through September, trail users can listen to live concert series at Buzzard's Glory Quarry. La Porte City holds the Festival of Trails in June, and the Cedar Rapids Freedom Festival is July 4th.

For tourism information, contact the Waterloo Convention & Visitors Bureau, P.O. Box 1587, Waterloo, IA 50704, (319) 233-8431; or Cedar Rapids Convention & Visitors Bureau, 119 1st Avenue SE, Cedar Rapids, IA 52406, (319) 398-5009.

EVANSDALE
Trailhead on River Road (I-380 exit 70): parking*, picnic tables
City facilities
Bike shop/repair (Waterloo)
Camping
City park
Groceries
Hospital (Waterloo)
Lodging (Waterloo)
Restaurants

GILBERTVILLE
Trailhead at E. Washburn Road 1mile east of Gilbertville: parking*, restrooms*, picnic tables, drinking water, trail passes/ maps/information, concessions
City facilities
City park
Groceries
Restaurant

LA PORTE CITY
Trailhead at Brandon Road and D48: parking*, restrooms*, drinking water, trail passes
City facilities
Camping
City park
Groceries
Lodging
Restaurants

McFARLANE PARK
Trailhead on King Road, 3 miles east of La Porte City.
Drinking water
Parking*

Picnic tables
Restrooms*
Shelter
Trail passes

BRANDON
Trailhead at south end of East Street: parking*, restrooms*, picnic tables, drinking water, trail passes
City facilities
Convenience store
Restaurants

URBANA
Trailhead off Brush Avenue: parking, restrooms, picnic tables, drinking water, shelter
City facilities
Camping
City park
Convenience store

CENTER POINT
Trailhead at East Washington Street: parking, restrooms*, picnic tables, drinking water, shelter
City facilities
City park
Groceries
Lodging
Restaurants

HIAWATHA
Trailhead at Boyson Road: parking*, restrooms*, trail maps/ information
City facilities
Bike shop/repair (Cedar Rapids)
Groceries
Lodging
Picnicking
Restaurants

*Handicap-accessible

HOURS: Open year-round, 6:00 a.m.-10:30 p.m. in Black Hawk and Buchanan Counties; 4:00 a.m.-10:30 p.m. in Linn and Benton Counties.
FEE: User fee required: $2.00/day or $5.00/year; $2.00/year for ages 11-16 and 65+; children under 11 are free. Trail passes are also available at local businesses.
TRAIL FACTS: Total miles: 52; **Miles completed:** Complete, except 1.5 mile gap just north of Urbana (to be completed in 1994); **Surfacing:** Crushed limestone
INFORMATION: Black Hawk County Conservation Board, 2410 W. Lone Tree Rd., Cedar Falls, Iowa 50613; (319) 266-0328 or Linn County Conservation Board, 1890 County Home Rd., Marion, Iowa 52302; (319) 398-3505

CHICHAQUA VALLEY TRAIL

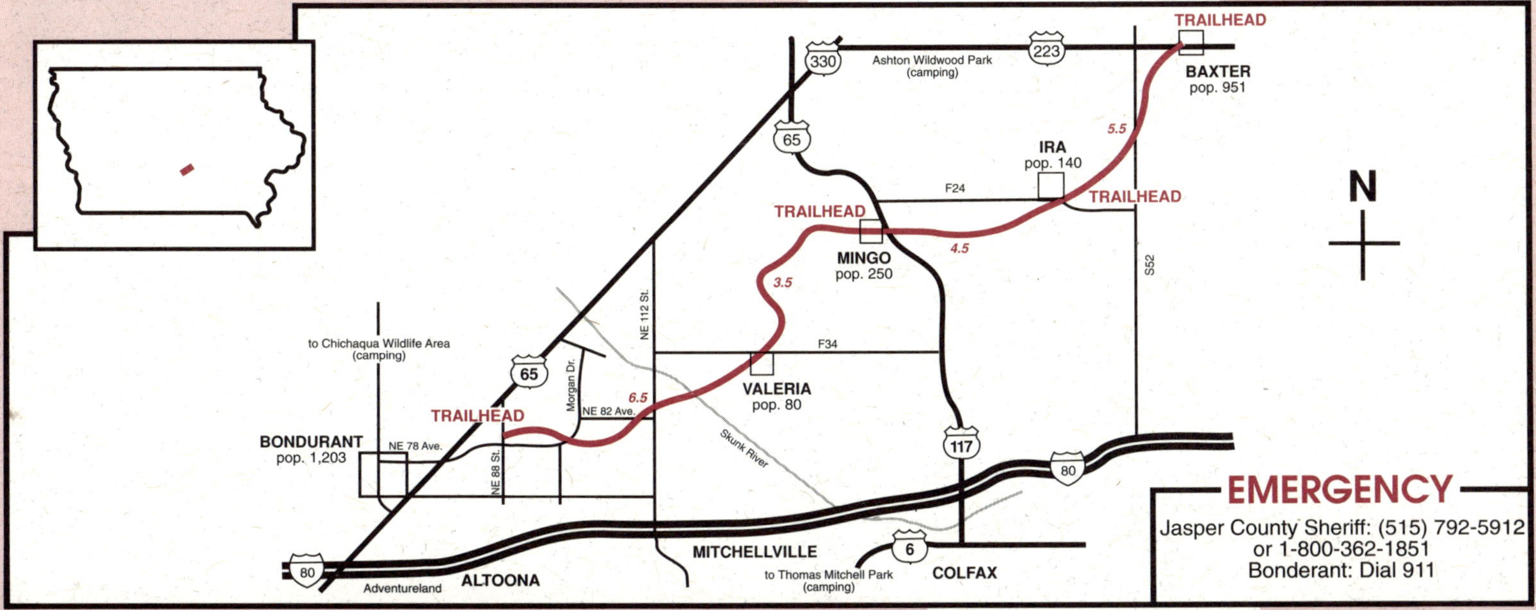

EMERGENCY
Jasper County Sheriff: (515) 792-5912
or 1-800-362-1851
Bondurant: Dial 911

Trailheads: Baxter, Ira/Mingo, Bondurant

Towns along the trail:
- BAXTER (pop. 951)
- IRA (pop. 140)
- MINGO (pop. 250)
- VALERIA (pop. 80)
- BONDURANT (pop. 1,203)
- COLFAX
- MITCHELLVILLE
- ALTOONA

Distances:
- Baxter to Ira: 5.5
- Ira to Mingo: 4.5
- Mingo to Valeria: 3.5
- Valeria to Bondurant: 6.5

Nearby features:
- Ashton Wildwood Park (camping)
- Thomas Mitchell Park (camping)
- Chichaqua Wildlife Area (camping)
- Adventureland
- Skunk River

Roads: 80, 330, 223, 65, 117, 6, S52, F24, F34, NE 112 St, NE 82 Ave, NE 88 St, NE 78 Ave, Morgan Dr

CHICHAQUA VALLEY TRAIL - Polk and Jasper Counties

The Chichaqua Valley Trail crosses the forested banks and timbered bluffs of the Skunk River. The Native American word "Chichaqua" was interpreted as "skunk" by the pioneers who settled in this area. The word probably refers to the odor of the wild onions that once grew along the river bank. Now, young trees stand along the trail that passes broad, rich farmland valleys, evidence of the passage of Iowa's last ice age glaciers.

The hiking and cycling itinerary allows visitors to discover small Iowa communities as well as many varieties of wildlife. The scenic terrain and diverse wildlife will suit the taste of any nature enthusiast.

A number of nearby attractions make this a family trail. The CVTCAT Ride, running the length of the trail, is held in mid-May, and Baxter Fun Days festivities take place in mid-June.

The Saylorville-Des Moines River Trail, seven miles west of Bondurant, allows easy access to the Des Moines metro area. Tourist information may be obtained by contacting the Des Moines Convention & Visitors Bureau, 309 Court Avenue, Des Moines, Iowa 50309; (515) 286-4960.

David Thoreson*

BAXTER
Trailhead on State Street: parking*, restrooms*, picnic tables
City facilities
Bread & breakfast
City park
Groceries
Medical clinic
Restaurants

IRA
Trailhead on County Rd. F24: parking*, restrooms*, picnic tables, shelter.
City facilities
Convenience store

MINGO
Trailhead on Hwy.117: parking*, restrooms*, picnic tables
City facilities
Camping
Information kiosk
Restaurant

BONDURANT
Trailhead 1 mile E. of town on NE 88th Street: parking*, restrooms*, picnic tables, trail maps/information
City facilities
City park
Groceries
Restaurant

*Handicap-accessible

HOURS: Open year-round, sunrise to sunset. **FEE:** No user fee required.
TRAIL FACTS: Total miles: 20; **Surfacing:** Crushed limestone; **Restrictions:** Snowmobiling allowed on trail only in Jasper County.
INFORMATION: Polk County Conservation Board, Jester Park, Granger, Iowa 50109; (515)999-2557 or Jasper County Conservation Board, County Annex Bldg., Newton, Iowa 50208; (515)792-9780.

CINDER PATH 6

EMERGENCY Dial 911

N

TRAILHEAD
DERBY pop. 171
306
2.5
1
9.5
H50
14
Charlton River
S56
RUSSELL
97
Red Haw Lake
Exercise Trail
TRAILHEAD
CHARITON pop. 5,116
Stephens Forest (13 miles NW)
S23
34
65
LUCAS

CINDER PATH - Lucas County

Scenic Cinder Path — Iowa's first rail-trail — winds its way through nine and one-half miles of the Chariton River valley in south central Iowa. Nestled between the two towns of Chariton and Derby, the trail is heavily lined with native Iowa timber and is also the peaceful home to wildflowers, prairie areas and wildlife. Sixteen wooden bridges, a covered bridge and a 20-foot lookout tower add to the charm of Cinder Path, named for its original cinder surface. Several rest stops with picnicking and primitive restroom facilities conveniently line the trail. A three and one-half mile segment of Cinder Path just west of Derby will be completed in 1994.

Adjoining Cinder Path north of Chariton's Business 34 is the Lucas County Conservation Exercise Trail. A mile and one-half in length, the exercise trail sports 13 stations, beginning with warm-up activities, accelerating to aerobic activities and ending with a cool-down.

For camping enthusiasts, Red Haw Lake just east of Chariton is the perfect backdrop for a peaceful night in the out-of-doors. The 300-acre park, equipped with a modern shower and toilet facility, also features a beach and boat launch. For more tourist information, contact the Chariton Chamber of Commerce, 104 N. Grand, Chariton, Iowa, 50049; (515)774-4059.

David Thoreson

CHARITON
Trailhead at west end of Business 34: parking*, picnic tables, trail maps/information
City facilities
Bike shop/repair
City park
Groceries
Hospital
Lodging
Restaurants

DERBY
Trailhead at east side of the grain elevator: parking, picnic tables
City facilities
City park
Restaurant

* Handicap-accessible

HOURS: Open year-round, sunrise to sunset.
FEE: No user fee required.
TRAIL FACTS: Total miles: 13; **Miles completed:** 9.5 (Derby to Chariton); **Surfacing:** Cinder
INFORMATION: Lucas County Conservation Board, Box 78, Chariton, Iowa 50049; (515) 774-4749

CLIVE GREENBELT TRAIL 7

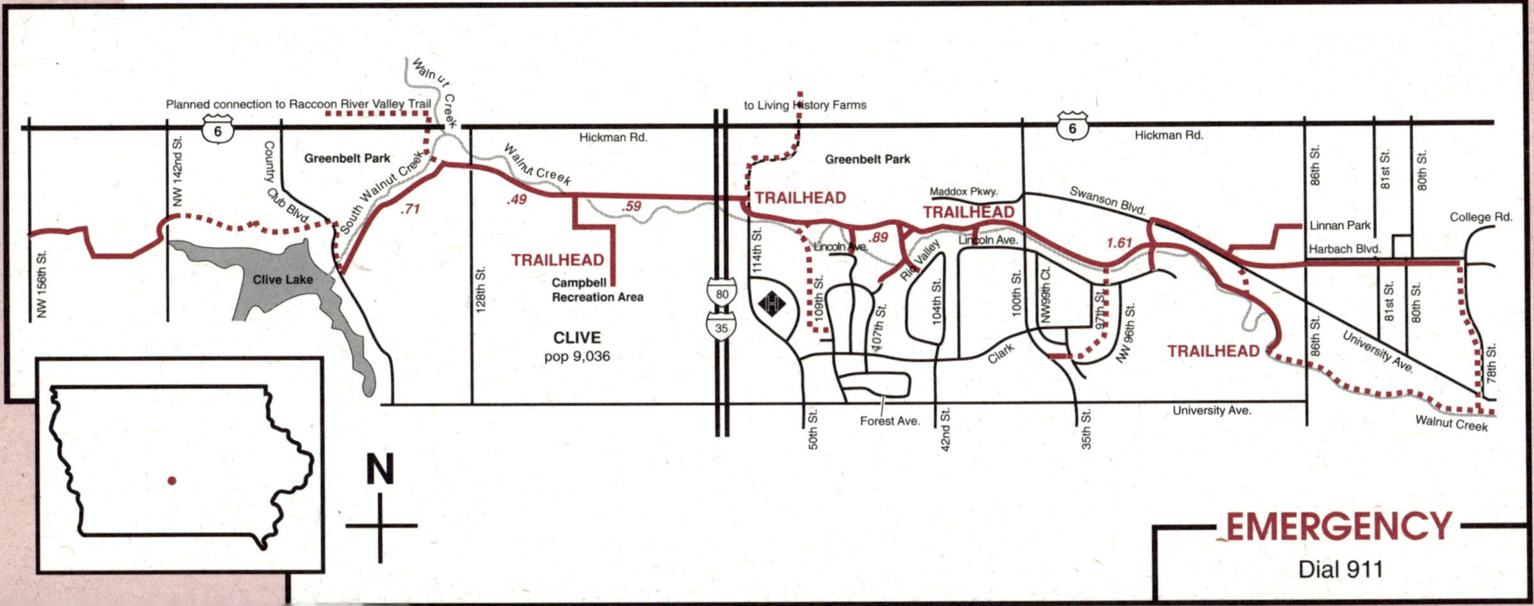

EMERGENCY

Dial 911

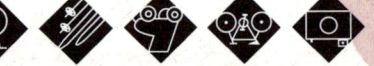

CLIVE GREENBELT TRAIL - Clive

This city greenbelt trail winds its way through scenic, heavily wooded areas. Along the trail, markers identify trees, shrubs and wildflowers as well as exercise stations. The trail links many parks and recreation areas. The Campbell Recreation Area, a new addition to the trail, contains softball fields, concessions, picnic areas, restrooms, tennis courts and a large playground featuring special handicap-accessible play equipment. A restored depot will also be relocated in this park.

There are a few sections of the trail that utilize streets or sidewalks. They include the section leading to Linnan Park, the segment between Country Club Boulevard and NW 142nd Street, and the section that runs along Harbach Boulevard to College Road.

During the year Clive has a number of festivals including the Winter Festival held in February, a running festival the third Saturday in May which uses part of the trail for the 5 and 10K races, and a summer festival the last weekend in June.

Living History Farms, located on the Hickman exit of I-35, north of the trail, traces the history of farming in Iowa. The 1876 Walnut Hill Victorian Mansion and re-created pioneer village show the day-to-day activities of early small town life. Another attraction is the Jordan House in West Des Moines, an 1850 mansion which was home to the first Walnut Township pioneer.

An extraordinary selection of lodging and restaurants exist near the trail. A listing of these amenities may be obtained by contacting the Des Moines Convention & Visitors Bureau, 309 Court Avenue, Des Moines, Iowa 50309; (515) 286-4960.

CLIVE
Trailhead at 1400 block of 86th Street: parking*, picnic tables
Trailhead on Maddox Parkway: parking*, restrooms*, drinking water
Trailhead on 114th Street: parking*
Trailhead at Campbell Recreation Area: parking*, restrooms*, playground*
City facilities
Bicycle shop/repair
City parks
Convenience stores
Groceries
Hospital
Lodging
Restaurants

*Handicap-accessible

HOURS: Open year-round, 6:00 a.m.-10:30 p.m.
FEE: No user fee required.
TRAIL FACTS: Total miles: 6.2; **Miles completed:** 5.7; **Surfacing:** Asphalt and fine gravel
INFORMATION: Clive Parks and Recreation Department, 9289 Swanson Boulevard, Clive, Iowa 50325; (515) 223-6230

COMET TRAIL 8

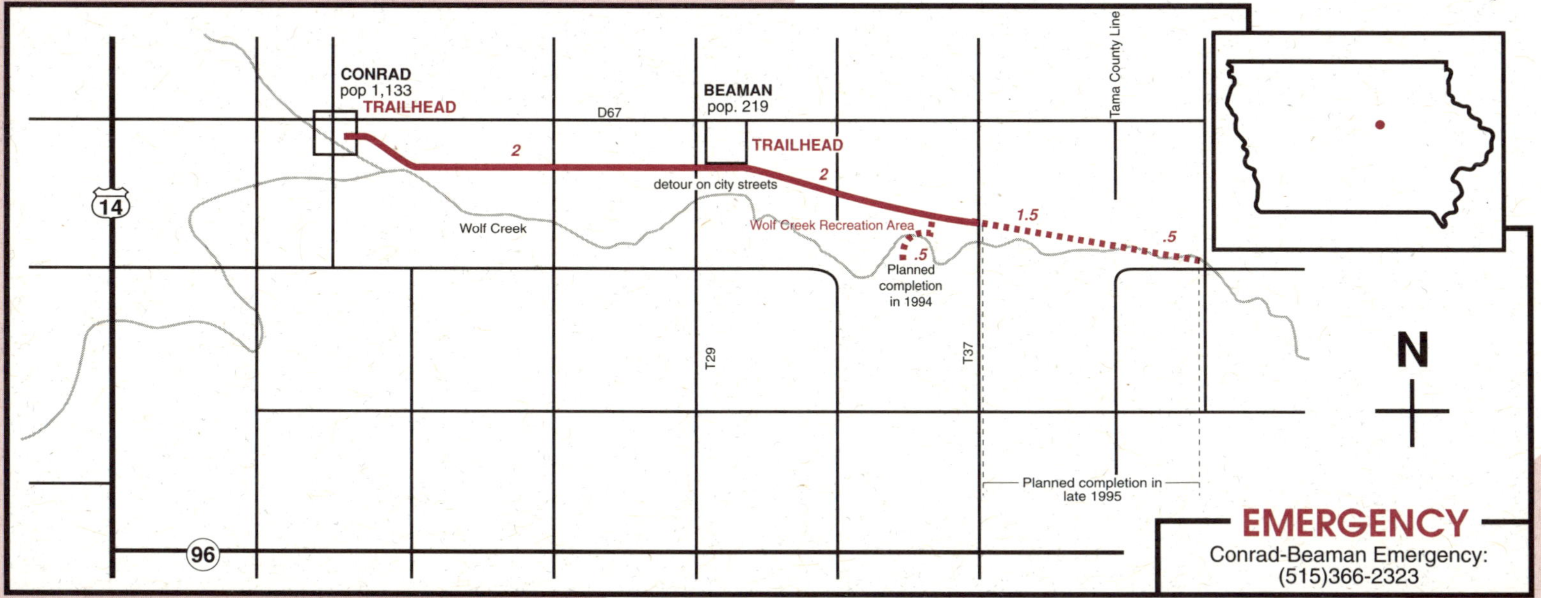

EMERGENCY
Conrad-Beaman Emergency:
(515)366-2323

CONRAD pop 1,133 — TRAILHEAD
BEAMAN pop. 219 — TRAILHEAD

- .5 — Planned completion in late 1995
- 1.5
- .5 — Planned completion in 1994
- Wolf Creek Recreation Area
- 2 — detour on city streets
- 2
- Wolf Creek

Tama County Line
T37
T29
D67
96
14

COMET TRAIL - Grundy County

In Grundy County's southeastern-most tip lies the Comet Trail, named after the BCL-UW High Comets. The trail is formed by a section of Chicago Northwestern line that travels through gently rolling hills, bits and pieces of prairie remnants, lively woodlands and brush, plus four train trestles.

The Wolf Creek Recreation Area provides peaceful camping and picnicking facilities, grass trails for hiking and a ball field, on a 93-acre woodland and recreational facility. A planned suspension bridge will eventually connect the park to Comet Trail. Until the bridge is completed, it will be necessary for trail users to travel a quarter mile on county gravel roads to reach the park entrance.

While you're in the area, stop by Grundy County's Pioneer Trail, less than eleven miles north of the Comet Trail. For more tourist information, contact the Grundy County Conservation Board listed below.

Bruce Morrison

CONRAD
Trailhead at south end of town on Alice Street: parking, picnic tables
City facilities
City park
Groceries
Medical clinic
Restaurants

BEAMAN
Trailhead at southeast corner of Beaman on county road: parking
City facilities
City park
Groceries
Restaurant

WOLF CREEK RECREATION AREA
Camping
Drinking water
Electricity
Parking
Picnic tables
Playground
Restrooms
Shelter

HOURS: Open year-round, sunrise to sunset. **FEE:** No user fee required.
TRAIL FACTS: Total miles: 6; **Miles completed:** 4 (Conrad to north Wolf Creek Area);
Surfacing: Crushed limestone
INFORMATION: Grundy County Conservation Board, P.O. Box 36, Morrison, Iowa 50657; (319) 345-2688

DICKINSON COUNTY SPINE TRAIL

DICKINSON COUNTY SPINE TRAIL - Dickinson County

The Dickinson County Spine Trail winds through Iowa's Great Lakes region, serving as "the spine" for future trails that eventually will be joined to it. The trail joins the four festive towns of Spirit Lake, Okoboji, Arnolds Park and Milford. With popular blue lakes, sandy beaches, specialty shops, golf courses, tennis courts and festivals throughout the seasons, the Spine Trail offers many interesting entertainment alternatives. The trail rambles through wildlife areas, along the shore of East Lake Okoboji and even through Okoboji's downtown area, truly giving trail users a diverse experience.

Future plans include extending the trail around Big Spirit Lake to Minnesota. Enjoy this unique trail, and if you need more tourist information, contact the Great Lakes Chamber of Commerce, Lakes Center Mall, Arnolds Park, Iowa 51331; (712) 332-2107.

David Thoreson

SPIRIT LAKE
Trailhead at 23rd Street & Keokuk: parking*, picnic tables
City facilities
Bed & breakfast
Camping
Groceries
Hospital
Restaurants

OKOBOJI
Trailhead 1/2 mile east off Hwy. 71, on Cartwright Road: parking*, picnic tables
City facilities
Camping
Groceries
Lodging
Restaurants

ARNOLDS PARK
Trailhead 1/4 mile off Hwy. 71, on Emerald Road: parking*, picnic tables
City Facilities
Bike shop/repair
Camping
Groceries
Lodging
Restaurants

MILFORD
Trailhead off of Hwy. 71: parking*, picnic tables
City facilities
Bike shop/repair
Groceries
Lodging
Restaurants

* Handicap-accessible

HOURS: Open year-round, no restrictive hours.
FEE: No user fee required.
TRAIL FACTS: Total miles: 10; **Surfacing:** Asphalt
INFORMATION: Dickinson County Conservation Board, 1013 Okoboji Avenue, Milford, Iowa 51351; (712) 338-4786

DUCK CREEK PARKWAY TRAIL & RIVERFRONT TRAIL

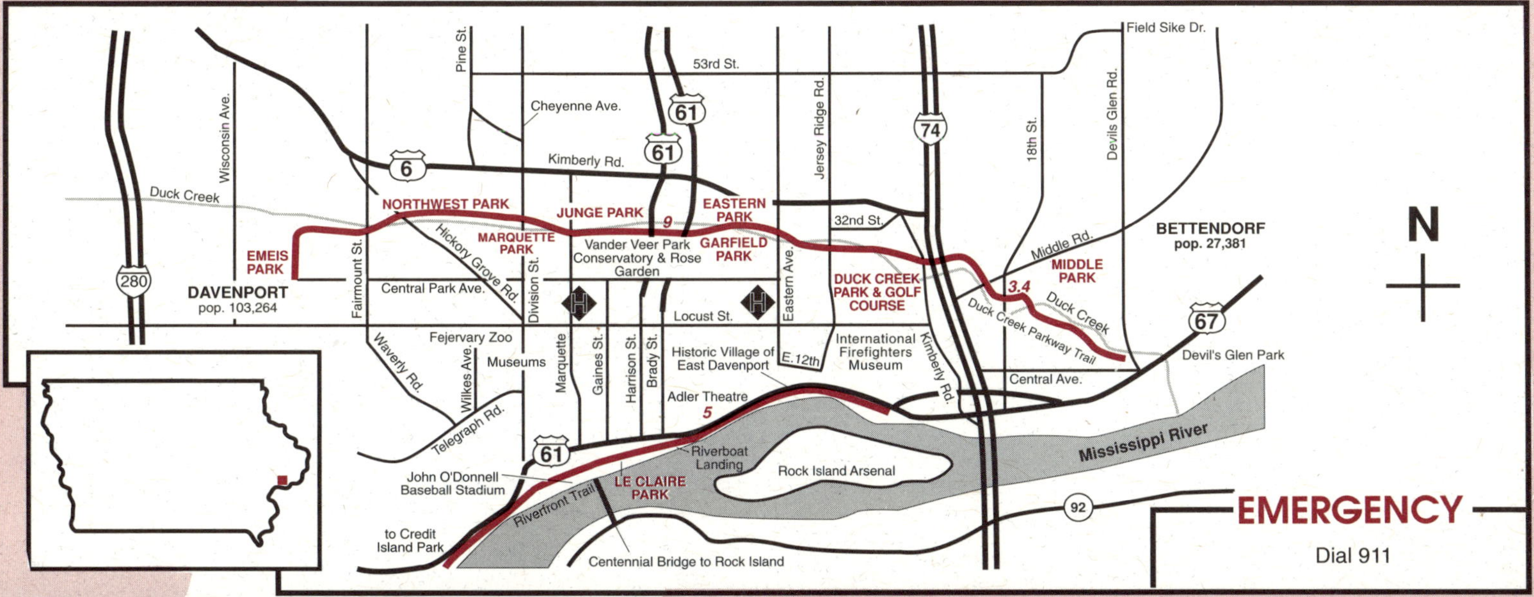

EMERGENCY Dial 911

DUCK CREEK PARKWAY TRAIL & RIVERFRONT TRAIL - Quad City

Duck Creek Parkway, serving as the lifeline of the Davenport/Bettendorf park and recreation system, is a 12-mile urban green belt located in one of Iowa's oldest cities. It provides a wide variety of scenic and recreational opportunities as it meanders through native woodlands, wetlands, urban housing areas, two golf courses and eight city parks. The asphalt/concrete surface extends over flat and gently rolling terrain, making it an ideal experience for all age groups. The multi-use trail follows the Duck Creek tributary from Emeis Park, in Davenport, to an area north of Devil's Glen Park, in Bettendorf.

The Riverfront Trail, connecting the historic village of East Davenport with other attractions, follows the Mississippi River from Mound Street to Credit Island Park. Plans include the extension of the trail to Bettendorf city limits and the addition of a segment that circles Credit Island Park.

The Quad City provides visitors with a variety of historical landmarks, fine dining, cultural opportunities and many other forms of entertainment. In Davenport, highlights include the Bix Beiderbecke Memorial Jazz Festival in late July and the Quad City Ride the River, a 20-mile riverfront family bike ride that includes a ferry ride over the river. Festivals and outdoor activites extend from spring through winter, and museums, art centers and botanical centers are numerous and well worth your time.

For more tourism information and a guide to the greater Quad City trails, contact the Quad City Convention & Visitors Bureau at P.O. Box 3097, Rock Island, Illinois 61204; (309) 788-7800 or 1-800-747-7800.

DAVENPORT
Trailheads:
Duck Creek Parkway trailheads within parks include parking, restrooms, picnic tables, shelter and drinking water. Riverfront Trail trailheads are located at Le Claire Park and Credit Island Park.
City facilities
Bed & breakfasts
Bike shop/repair
City parks
Camping
Golf courses
Groceries
Hospitals
Hotels/motels
Restaurants

BETTENDORF
Trailheads:
Parking is available on the street. Restrooms, picnic tables, shelters and drinking water can be found at Middle Park.
City facilities
Bed & breakfasts
Bike shop/repair
Camping
City parks
Groceries
Hotels/motels
Restaurants

HOURS: Open year-round, no restrictive hours.   **FEE:** No user fee required.
TRAIL FACTS: Total miles: Duck Creek Parkway: 12.4 miles; Riverfront Trail: 5 miles completed;
Surfacing: Asphalt and concrete
INFORMATION: Davenport Park & Recreation, 2816 Eastern Ave., Davenport, Iowa 52803; (319) 326-7812 or Davenport Levee Commission, City Hall, Davenport, Iowa 52801; (319) 326-7765

EAST RIVER BIKE TRAIL

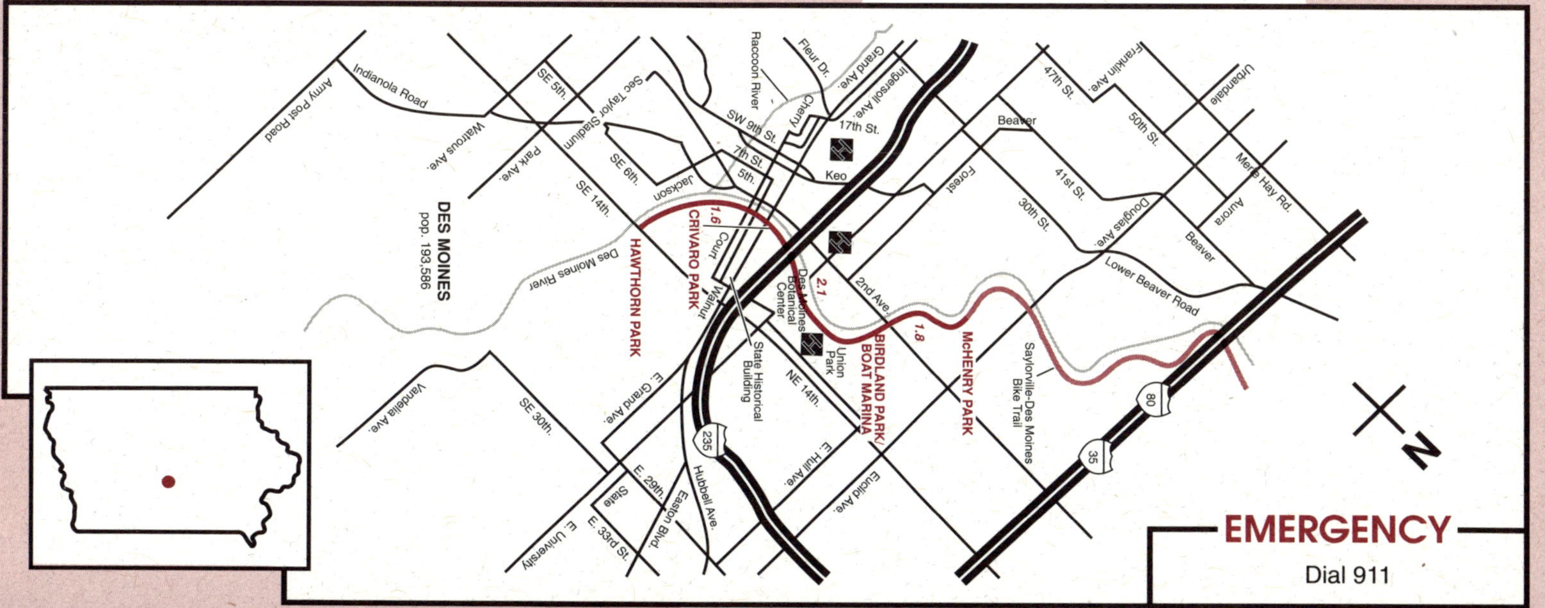

EMERGENCY Dial 911

11

DUCK CREEK PARKWAY TRAIL & RIVERFRONT TRAIL - Quad City

Duck Creek Parkway, serving as the lifeline of the Davenport/Bettendorf park and recreation system, is a 12-mile urban green belt located in one of Iowa's oldest cities. It provides a wide variety of scenic and recreational opportunities as it meanders through native woodlands, wetlands, urban housing areas, two golf courses and eight city parks. The asphalt/concrete surface extends over flat and gently rolling terrain, making it an ideal experience for all age groups. The multi-use trail follows the Duck Creek tributary from Emeis Park, in Davenport, to an area north of Devil's Glen Park, in Bettendorf.

The Riverfront Trail, connecting the historic village of East Davenport with other attractions, follows the Mississippi River from Mound Street to Credit Island Park. Plans include the extension of the trail to Bettendorf city limits and the addition of a segment that circles Credit Island Park.

The Quad City provides visitors with a variety of historical landmarks, fine dining, cultural opportunities and many other forms of entertainment. In Davenport, highlights include the Bix Beiderbecke Memorial Jazz Festival in late July and the Quad City Ride the River, a 20-mile riverfront family bike ride that includes a ferry ride over the river. Festivals and outdoor activites extend from spring through winter, and museums, art centers and botanical centers are numerous and well worth your time.

For more tourism information and a guide to the greater Quad City trails, contact the Quad City Convention & Visitors Bureau at P.O. Box 3097, Rock Island, Illinois 61204; (309) 788-7800 or 1-800-747-7800.

DAVENPORT
Trailheads:
Duck Creek Parkway trailheads within parks include parking, restrooms, picnic tables, shelter and drinking water. Riverfront Trail trailheads are located at Le Claire Park and Credit Island Park.
City facilities
Bed & breakfasts
Bike shop/repair
City parks
Camping
Golf courses
Groceries
Hospitals
Hotels/motels
Restaurants

BETTENDORF
Trailheads:
Parking is available on the street. Restrooms, picnic tables, shelters and drinking water can be found at Middle Park.
City facilities
Bed & breakfasts
Bike shop/repair
Camping
City parks
Groceries
Hotels/motels
Restaurants

HOURS: Open year-round, no restrictive hours. **FEE:** No user fee required.
TRAIL FACTS: Total miles: Duck Creek Parkway: 12.4 miles; Riverfront Trail: 5 miles completed;
Surfacing: Asphalt and concrete
INFORMATION: Davenport Park & Recreation, 2816 Eastern Ave., Davenport, Iowa 52803; (319) 326-7812 or Davenport Levee Commission, City Hall, Davenport, Iowa 52801; (319) 326-7765

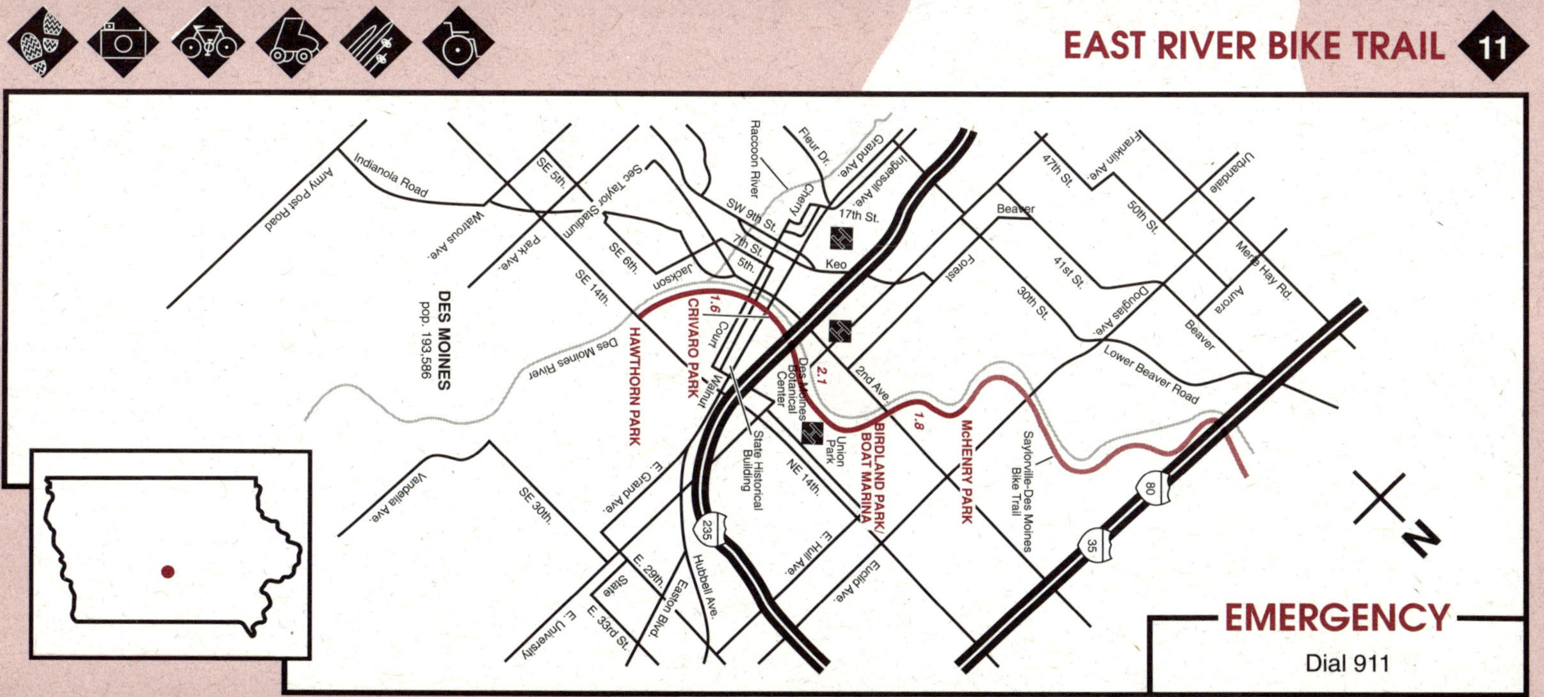

EAST RIVER BIKE TRAIL   11

EMERGENCY
Dial 911

EAST RIVER BIKE TRAIL - Des Moines

Although primarily located in an urban setting, the East River Bike Trail is accented with many natural features. It follows the river through the city, passing the new Sec Taylor Baseball Stadium and the old Riverview Park, now a natural wetland. The Des Moines River corridor is habitat for a variety of birds, including eagles and common waterfowl. The north end of East River Bike Trail connects to Saylorville-Des Moines River Trail.

The trail contrasts the new and old. At various points along the trail, the visitor is provided with panoramic views of the Des Moines River as well as a dramatic view of the Des Moines skyline. A historical marker at Crivaro Park commemorates an early ferry crossing on the Des Moines River. During the summer months, "The Spirit of Des Moines" docks at the Botanical Center and takes passengers on dinner cruises up the Des Moines River.

In June, Des Moines celebrates its heritage at the Two Rivers Festival which includes excellent jazz music, arts, crafts and fireworks. Des Moines is host to a myriad of other cultural events; contact the Des Moines Convention & Visitors Bureau for more tourist information: 601 Locust, Des Moines, Iowa 50309; (515) 286-4960.

Bob Coyle

DES MOINES
Trailhead at McHenry Park (8th & Oak Park Ave.): parking*, restrooms, picnic tables, drinking water, shelter
Trailhead at Birdland Park (Birdland Drive & Saylor Road): parking, restrooms, picnic tables, drinking water, phones, boating
Trailhead at Crivaro Park (E. 1st & Grand Ave.): picnic tables
Trailhead at Hawthorn Park (SE l4th & Railroad Ave.): parking*, restrooms*, picnic tables, drinking water, basketball court, softball field
City facilities
Bed & breakfasts
Bicycle shop/repair/rental
Camping
City parks
Groceries
Hospital
Hotels/motels
Restaurants

* Handicap-accessible

HOURS: Open year-round except in snow or ice conditions. No restrictive hours.
FEE: No user fee required.
TRAIL FACTS: Total miles: 5.5; **Surfacing:** Asphalt
INFORMATION: Des Moines Parks & Recreation, 3226 University Ave., Des Moines, Iowa 50311; (5l5) 237-1386

FORT DODGE NATURE TRAIL 12

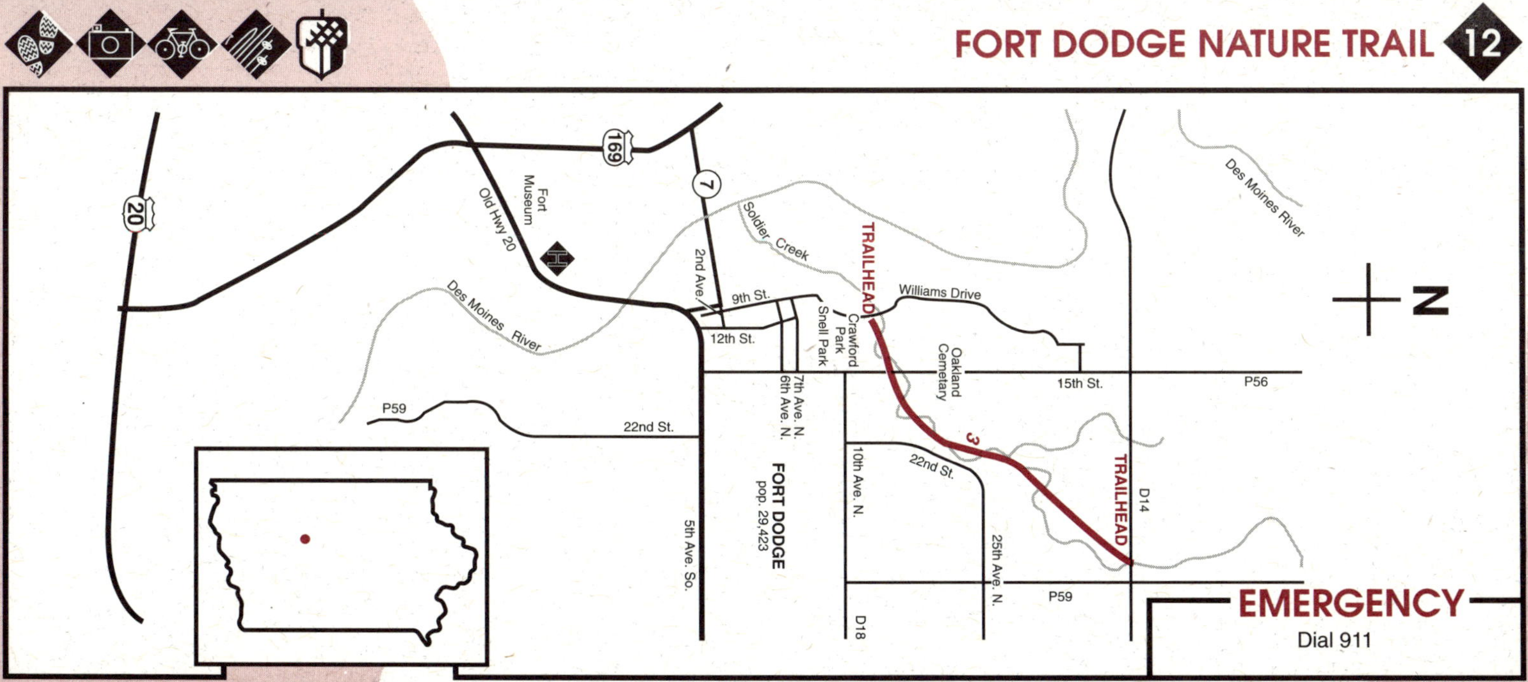

FORT DODGE NATURE TRAIL - Fort Dodge

The popular Fort Dodge Nature Trail offers natural beauty and diverse recreation year-round. The trail follows the Chicago Northwestern railbed for three miles, taking users from city parks to countryside on a tour that packs a variety of scenery in an easily covered distance. The diverse landscape along the trail ranges from forested areas that create a canopy effect overhead, to brush areas filled with wildlife, to clearings that afford views of nearby rolling hills. Several bridges on the trail span segments of the winding Soldier Creek, and trail users can pause for a "rest stop" at a small shelter with benches.

In the spring and summer a profusion of wildflowers decorates sections of the trail, providing an extra treat for visitors. In the winter, visitors can use the trail for cross-country skiing and winter hiking. Winter activities also include sledding on the hills of Crawford Park.

Along with the scenery and recreation, the trail features historic attractions. Oakland Cemetery has graves dating back to the early 1800s, and the stone cabins in Snell Park were built by the Workers Progress Association (WPA) after WWII.

The city, itself, is historically significant. The original fort, built near the Des Moines River, is gone now, but another has been re-established at the historic Fort Museum. The fort includes a pioneer village containing a replica of the Cardiff Giant, a famous hoax carved from a piece of Fort Dodge gypsum. A unique collection of pioneer, military and Native American exhibits are also open to the public.

For more information on historic sites, recreation and other attractions in Fort Dodge, contact the Fort Dodge Chamber of Commerce, 1406 Central Ave., Fort Dodge, Iowa 50501; (515) 955-5500.

FORT DODGE
Trailhead on Williams Drive: parking*, restrooms*, picnic tables, drinking water, shelter
Trailhead at County Road D14: parking
City facilities
Bike shop/repair
Camping
City parks
Golf course
Groceries
Hospital
Lodging
Restaurants
Swimming pool

*Handicap-accessible

HOURS: Open year-round, 4:30 a.m.-10:30 p.m.
FEE: No user fee required.
TRAIL FACTS: Total miles: 3; **Surfacing:** Cinder
INFORMATION: Fort Dodge Parks Department, 819 First Avenue South, Fort Dodge, Iowa 50501; (515) 576-7237

FRANKLIN GROVE HERITAGE TRAIL 13

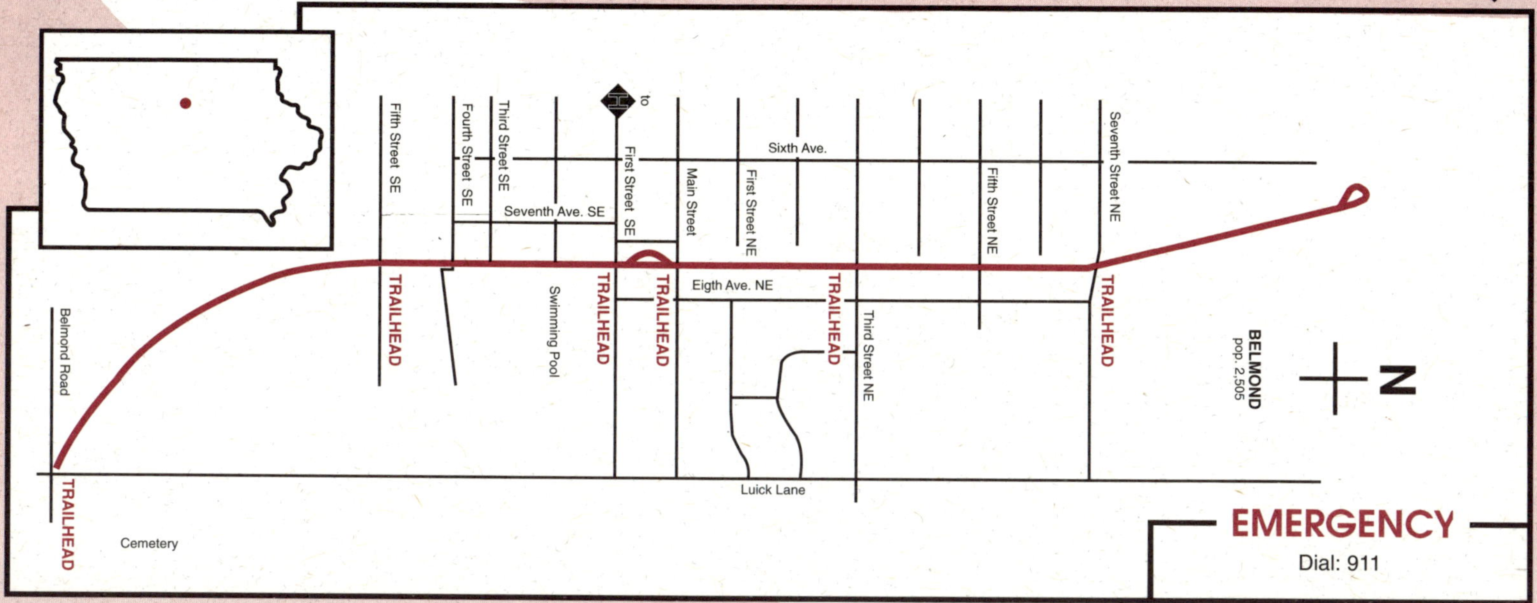

EMERGENCY

Dial: 911

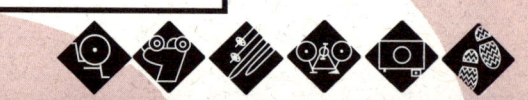

FORT DODGE NATURE TRAIL - Fort Dodge

The popular Fort Dodge Nature Trail offers natural beauty and diverse recreation year-round. The trail follows the Chicago Northwestern railbed for three miles, taking users from city parks to countryside on a tour that packs a variety of scenery in an easily covered distance. The diverse landscape along the trail ranges from forested areas that create a canopy effect overhead, to brush areas filled with wildlife, to clearings that afford views of nearby rolling hills. Several bridges on the trail span segments of the winding Soldier Creek, and trail users can pause for a "rest stop" at a small shelter with benches.

In the spring and summer a profusion of wildflowers decorates sections of the trail, providing an extra treat for visitors. In the winter, visitors can use the trail for cross-country skiing and winter hiking. Winter activities also include sledding on the hills of Crawford Park.

Along with the scenery and recreation, the trail features historic attractions. Oakland Cemetery has graves dating back to the early 1800s, and the stone cabins in Snell Park were built by the Workers Progress Association (WPA) after WWII.

The city, itself, is historically significant. The original fort, built near the Des Moines River, is gone now, but another has been re-established at the historic Fort Museum. The fort includes a pioneer village containing a replica of the Cardiff Giant, a famous hoax carved from a piece of Fort Dodge gypsum. A unique collection of pioneer, military and Native American exhibits are also open to the public.

For more information on historic sites, recreation and other attractions in Fort Dodge, contact the Fort Dodge Chamber of Commerce, 1406 Central Ave., Fort Dodge, Iowa 50501; (515) 955-5500.

FORT DODGE
Trailhead on Williams Drive: parking*, restrooms*, picnic tables, drinking water, shelter
Trailhead at County Road D14: parking
City facilities
Bike shop/repair
Camping
City parks
Golf course
Groceries
Hospital
Lodging
Restaurants
Swimming pool

*Handicap-accessible

HOURS: Open year-round, 4:30 a.m.-10:30 p.m.
FEE: No user fee required.
TRAIL FACTS: Total miles: 3;   **Surfacing:** Cinder
INFORMATION: Fort Dodge Parks Department, 819 First Avenue South, Fort Dodge, Iowa 50501; (515) 576-7237

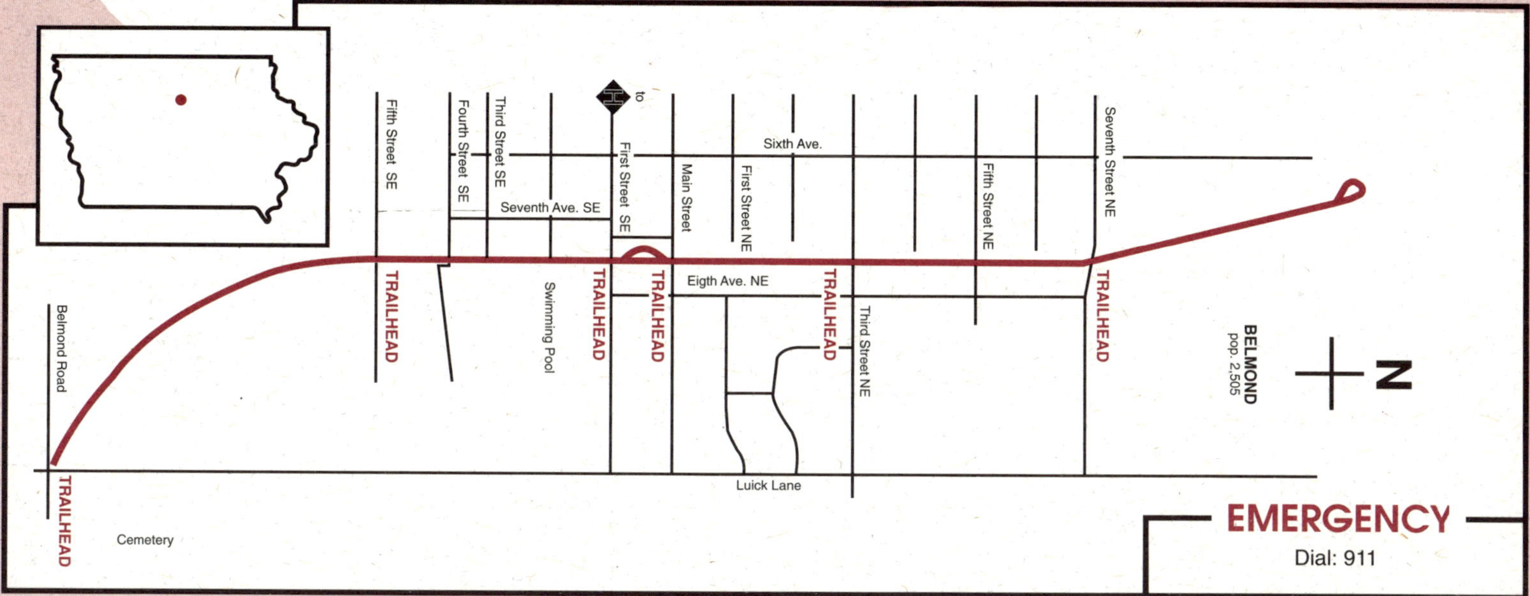

EMERGENCY

Dial: 911

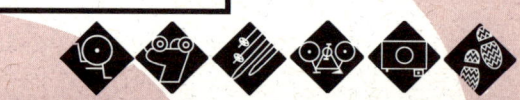

FRANKLIN GROVE HERITAGE TRAIL - Belmond

The Franklin Grove trail, built on the abandoned railbed of the Rock Island Railroad, joins the residential section of Belmond to rural areas north and south of the town.

The journey on the north end of the trail takes visitors through a prairie area with native grasses and abundant prairie wildlife. Plans for the prairie provide for the reintroduction of prairie flowers in 1994. The trail becomes park-like through the residential area at the middle of the trail. This part of the trail is landscaped with trees, shrubs, and flowers, and it features limestone benches for resting.

At the southern end of the trail, the landscape changes to scenic brush and woodland teeming with a variety of birds and wildlife. Belmond's first pioneers settled in this area and named it "Franklin Grove." This piece of Belmond history is preserved in the trail name. Another historic area is Belmond's cemetery, which was established in 1856. It can be found at the south trailhead at Luick Lane South and Belmond Road.

For tourism information, contact the Belmond Chamber of Commerce, 112 2nd Ave. NE, Belmond, Iowa 50421; (515) 444-3937.

Ty Smedes

BELMOND
Trailhead at Luick Lane South and Belmond Road: parking*
Trailhead at 5th Street SE: parking*
Trailhead at 1st Street SE: parking*, swimming pool (open during summer months) restrooms*, phones, drinking water, picnic tables, shelter, concessions
Trailhead at Main Street: parking*
Trailhead at 3rd Street NE: parking*
Trailhead at 5th Street NE: parking*
Trailhead at 7th Street NE: parking*
City facilities
Bike repair
City parks
Groceries
Hospital
Lodging
Swimming pool

*Handicap-accessible

HOURS: Open year-round, no restrictive hours.
FEE: No user fee required.
TRAIL FACTS: Total miles: 1.8; **Surfacing:** Asphalt
INFORMATION: Belmond City Hall, 112 2nd Avenue NE, Belmond, Iowa 50421; (515) 444-3386

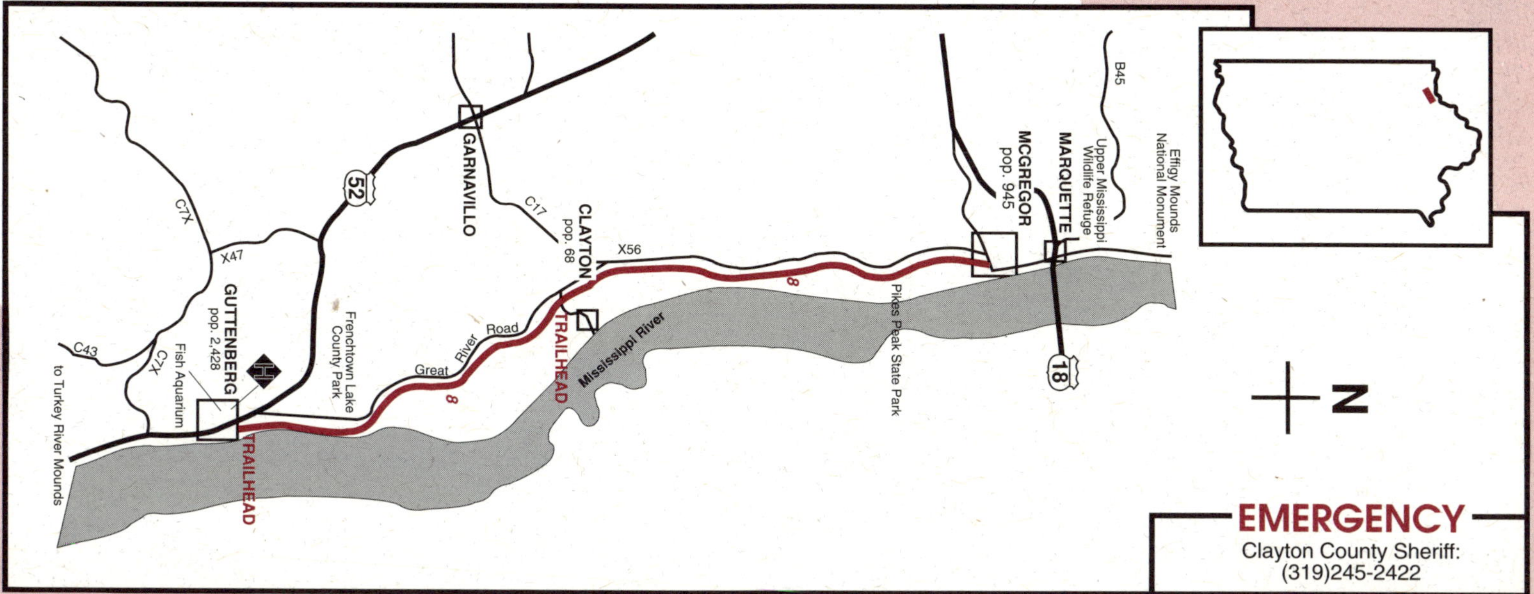

GREAT RIVER ROAD TRAIL 14

EMERGENCY
Clayton County Sheriff: (319) 245-2422

GREAT RIVER ROAD TRAIL - Clayton County

Oak and maple forests, cold water streams, bright red barns and soaring eagles are just a few appealing sights to behold on the Mississippi bluffland's Great River Road Trail. Sixteen miles of concrete trail takes you through what some consider Iowa's most beautiful landscape. This trail, which lies on the extended shoulders of County Road X56, is one of Iowa's steepest and most challenging trails. The three quaint river towns of Guttenburg, Clayton and McGregor add much charm to the experience with their hometown cafes and shops. Pikes Peak State Park, the Upper Mississippi Wildlife Refuge, the Effigy Mounds National Monument and nearby Yellow River Forest will give you the opportunity to experience the majesty of Iowa's Mississippi River blufflands.

Local festivals add to the trail experience. Guttenburg hosts Dairy Days in June and Fall Celebration in October. McGregor holds its well-known Art Festival twice each year in June and October. Good luck mastering this hilly terrain, and if you would like more tourist information, contact the McGregor Chamber of Commerce, McGregor, Iowa 52157; (319) 873-2186.

Herbert Lange

GUTTENBURG
Trailhead north of Guttenburg, off the Great River Road: parking*, restrooms*, picnic tables, phones, drinking water
City facilities
Bed & breakfast
Camping
City park
County park
Groceries
Hospital
Hotel/motel
Information center
Public showers
Restaurants

CLAYTON
Trailhead 1 mile east, off the Great River Road: parking

City Facilities:
Bed & breakfast
Camping
Restaurants

PIKES PEAK STATE PARK
Camping
Parking
Picnicking
Restrooms
Drinking water

MCGREGOR
City facilities
Bed & breakfast
Camping
City park
Groceries
Information center
Restaurants
State park

*Handicap-accessible

HOURS: Open year-round, no restrictive hours.
FEE: No user fee required.
TRAIL FACTS: Total miles: 16; **Surfacing:** Concrete
INFORMATION: Clayton County Conservation Board, RR 2 Box 65-A, Elkader, Iowa 52043; (319) 245-1516

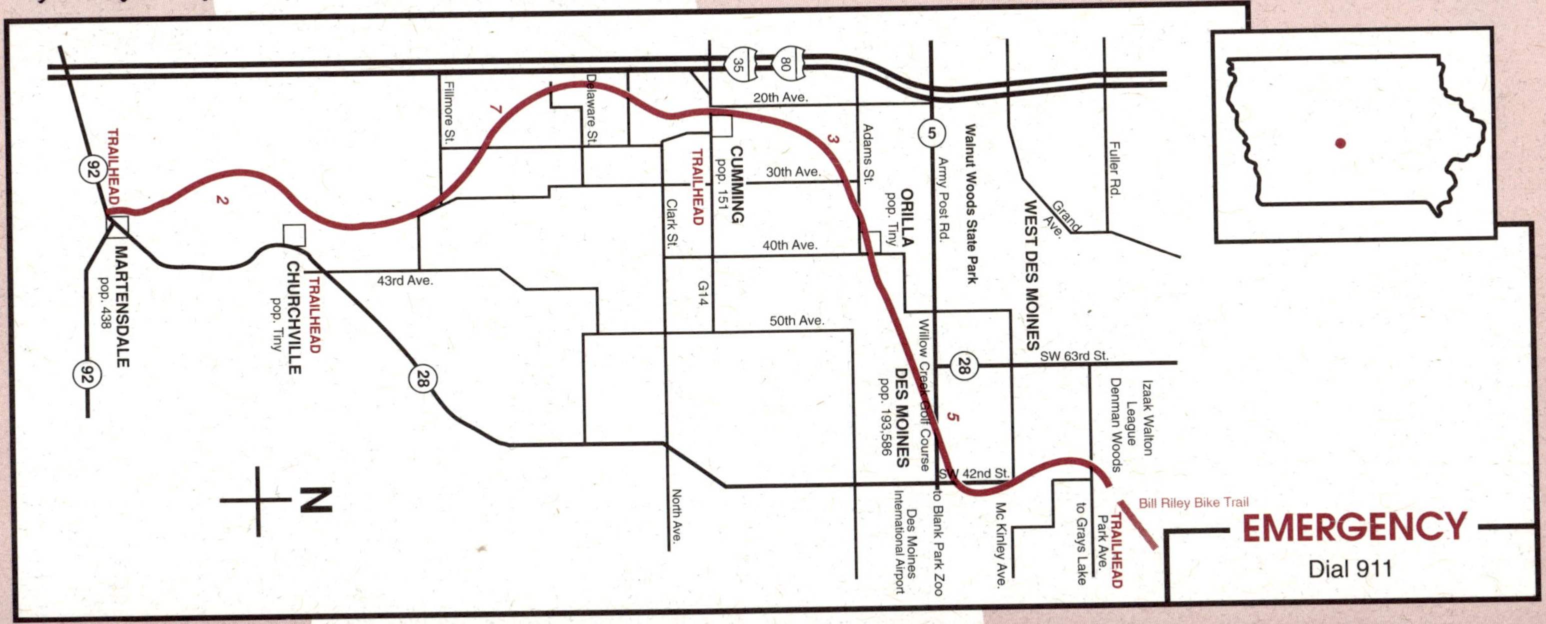

GREAT WESTERN TRAIL   15

EMERGENCY Dial 911

- TRAILHEAD Park Ave. to Grays Lake
- Bill Riley Bike Trail
- Mc Kinley Ave.
- to Blank Park Zoo
- Des Moines International Airport
- Izaak Walton League Denman Woods
- SW 63rd St.
- SW 42nd St.
- DES MOINES pop. 193,586
- Willow Creek Golf Course
- 28
- North Ave.
- 5
- 50th Ave.
- WEST DES MOINES
- Fuller Rd.
- Grand Ave.
- Army Post Rd.
- Walnut Woods State Park
- ORILLA pop. Tiny
- Adams St.
- 40th Ave.
- G14
- Clark St.
- 28
- TRAILHEAD CHURCHVILLE pop. Tiny
- 43rd Ave.
- 30th Ave.
- CUMMING pop. 151
- TRAILHEAD
- 3
- Delaware St.
- 7
- Fillmore St.
- 2
- TRAILHEAD
- 92
- MARTENSDALE pop. 438
- 20th Ave.
- 80
- 35
- 5

GREAT WESTERN TRAIL
- Polk and Warren Counties

This conservation-recreation trail was once part of the Chicago Northwestern, an extensive railway network in Iowa. Preserved as a transportation corridor, the trail has retained good examples of Iowa vegetation from 150 years past.

The Great Western Trail is a relatively flat, multi-purpose trail, perfect for bicycling, walking, studying nature and taking photographs. Rich meadows are alive with wildflowers, prairie grasses, songbirds, pheasants, hawks and a fine assortment of trees. Those with a quiet step and watchful eye will also observe an elusive fox, coyote or deer. Farm ponds, the North River and several meandering streams are evidence of the natural pastoral diversity of the area. A portion of the trail in Martensdale is paved with asphalt, making it suitable for skating. At the Des Moines trailhead, trail users can move on to the nearby Bill Riley Bike Trail.

For information on the area's special cultural attractions, contact the Des Moines Convention & Visitors Bureau, 309 Court Avenue, Des Moines, Iowa 50309; (515) 286-4960.

Bob Coyle

DES MOINES
Trailhead near Izaak Walton League Chapter House, 4343 Valley Drive: parking*, restrooms
City facilities
Bike shop/repair/rental
Camping
City parks
Groceries
Hospitals
Lodging
Restaurants

CUMMING
Trailhead 1 mile east of I-35 on County Road G14: parking*

City facilities
City park
Groceries
Restaurants

CHURCHVILLE
Trailhead 1 mile west of Hwy. 28 & Harrison Street: parking

MARTENSDALE
Trailhead 2 miles east of I-35 off Hwy. 28 at Inwood St.; parking*, restrooms*, shelter, drinking water
City facilities
Groceries
City park
Restaurants

*Handicap-accessible

HOURS: Open-year round, sunrise to sunset. **FEE:** No user fee required.
TRAIL FACTS: Total miles: 16.5; **Surfacing:** Crushed limestone; asphalt near Martensdale
INFORMATION: Polk County Conservation Board, Jester Park, Granger, Iowa 50109; (515) 999-2557 or Warren County Conservation Board, 1565 118th Avenue, Indianola, Iowa 50125; (515) 961-6169

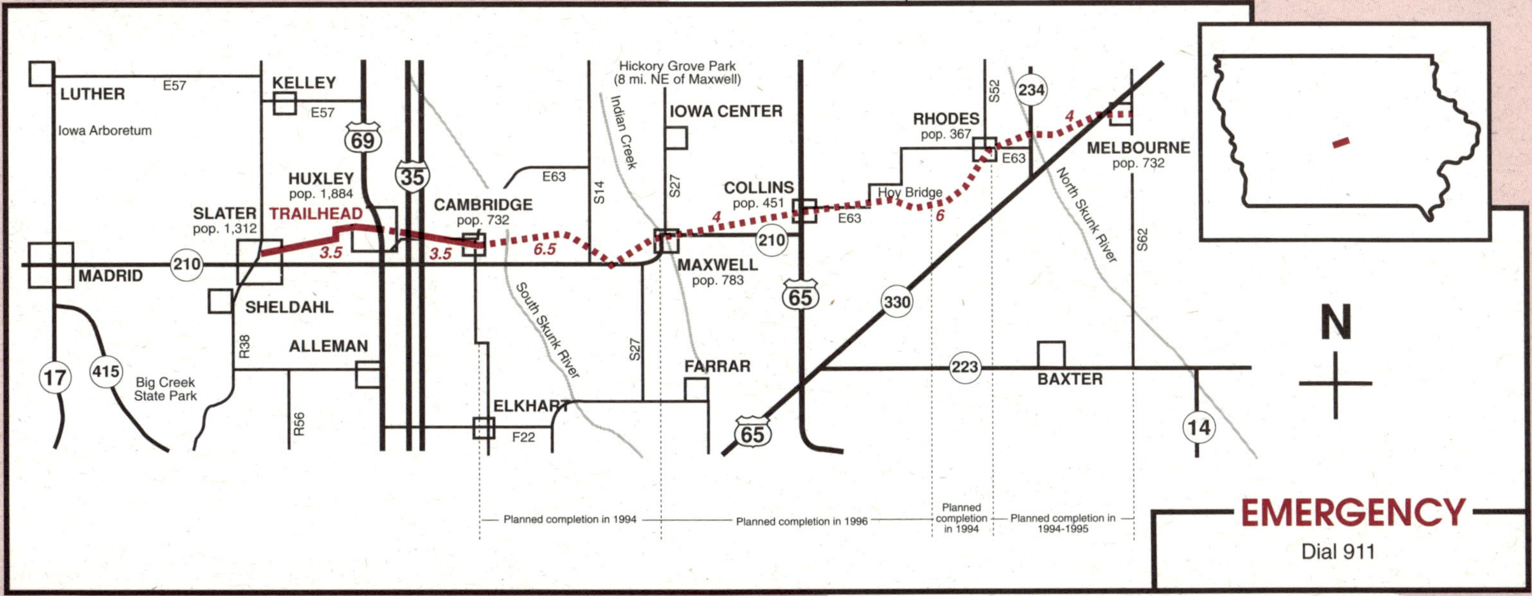

HEART OF IOWA NATURE TRAIL

16

EMERGENCY
Dial 911

HEART OF IOWA NATURE TRAIL
- Story and Marshall Counties

Rich river valleys, lively woodlands and quality prairie remnants are all available on the Heart of Iowa Nature Trail. In Story County, trail users will find significant prairie remnants east of Slater, a pioneer cemetery and historical museum in Maxwell, heavily wooded tracts near Cambridge and Maxwell and two wetland areas west of Cambridge.

Further east in Marshall County, near Rhodes, you'll travel over the Hoy Bridge, a unique, massive concrete arch bridge built in 1912 to accommodate a double railroad over Clear Creek. The structure, 212 feet in length and 60 feet in height, is an impressive frame for the picturesque Clear Creek valley lying beyond.

Future plans include connecting the west portion of the trail to the existing Saylorville Trail in Des Moines and the east trail portion to Chichaqua Valley Trail, making a 100-mile loop in central Iowa.

For tourism information, contact Slater City Hall, 105 Green St., Slater, Iowa 50244; (515) 685-2531 or the Story County Conservation Board listed below.

SLATER
Trailhead
NE of Slater on County Road R38: parking*, restrooms, drinking water, picnic tables, shelter, trail maps/information, arboretum
City facilities
City park
Groceries
Restaurants

HUXLEY
(Trailhead planned)
City facilities
Bike rental
City park
Groceries
Restaurants

CAMBRIDGE
(Trailhead planned)
City facilities
City park
Convenience store

MAXWELL
(Trailhead planned for Maxwell City Park along Indian Creek will include restrooms, shelter, drinking water and camping.)
City facilities
Camping
City park
Groceries
Restaurant

COLLINS
(Trailhead planned)
City facilities
Camping (8 miles north)
City park
Convenience store
Restaurant

RHODES
(Trailhead planned at South end of Main Street will include parking only.)
City facilities
City park

MELBOURNE
City facilities
Convenience store
Parking
Picnicking
Restaurant

* Handicap-accessible

HOURS: Open year-round, 5:00 a.m.-10:30 p.m.   **FEE:** No user fee at this time.
TRAIL FACTS: **Total miles**: 32 (upon completion in 2000);   **Miles completed**: 7;   **Surfacing**: Crushed limestone;
Restrictions: Equestrian use not allowed on city streets.
INFORMATION: Story County Conservation Board, McFarland Park, R. R. 2, Box 272V, Ames, Iowa 50010; (515) 232-2516 or Marshall County Conservation Board, 1302 E. Olive St., Marshalltown, Iowa 50158; (515) 754-6303

HERITAGE TRAIL 17

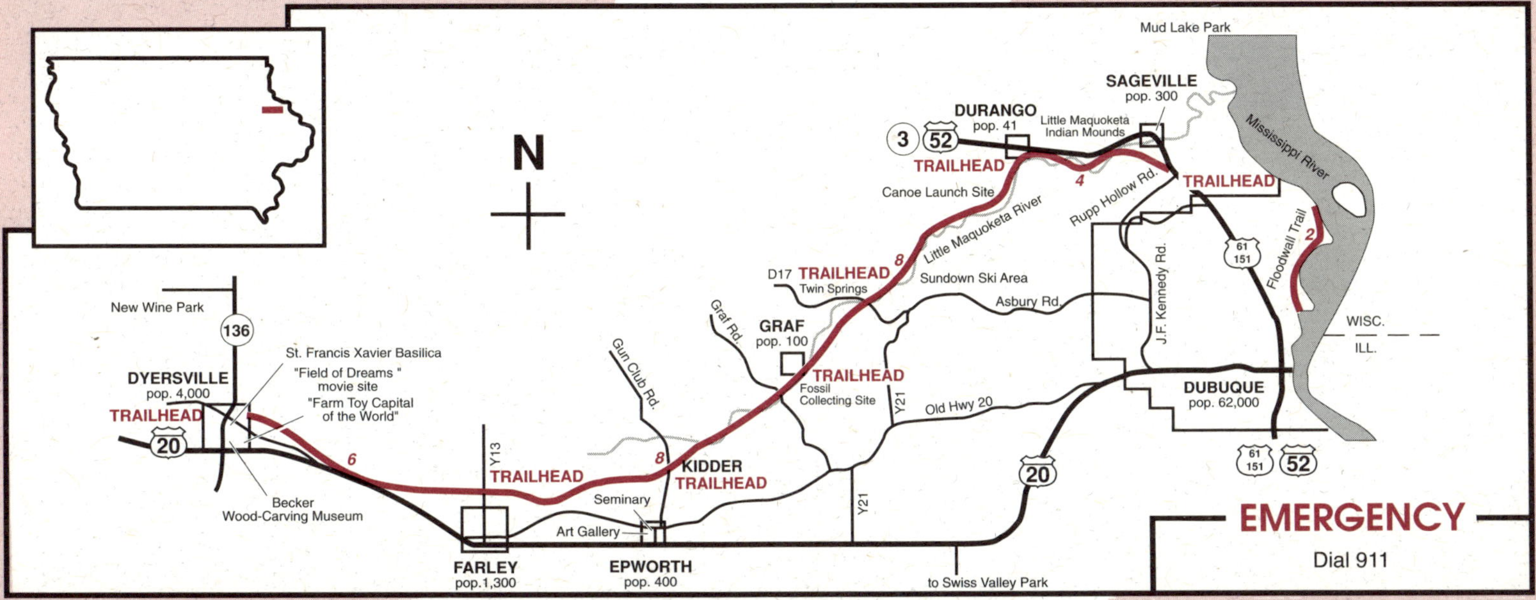

EMERGENCY Dial 911

Towns & Populations
- DUBUQUE pop. 62,000
- FARLEY pop. 1,300
- EPWORTH pop. 400
- DYERSVILLE pop. 4,000
- GRAF pop. 100
- DURANGO pop. 41
- SAGEVILLE pop. 300

Trailheads
- TRAILHEAD (Dyersville, Hwy 20)
- KIDDER TRAILHEAD
- TRAILHEAD (Graf)
- TRAILHEAD (near Twin Springs)
- TRAILHEAD (Durango, Hwy 52/3)
- TRAILHEAD (Sageville)

Roads
- 20, 151, 61, 52, 136, 41
- Y21, Y13, D17
- Old Hwy 20
- J.F. Kennedy Rd.
- Asbury Rd.
- Gun Club Rd.
- Graf Rd.
- Rupp Hollow Rd.

Points of Interest
- Becker Wood-Carving Museum
- "Farm Toy Capital of the World"
- "Field of Dreams" movie site
- St. Francis Xavier Basilica
- New Wine Park
- Art Gallery
- Seminary
- Fossil Collecting Site
- Sundown Ski Area
- Twin Springs
- Canoe Launch Site
- Little Maquoketa Indian Mounds
- Little Maquoketa River
- Mud Lake Park
- Floodwall Trail
- Mississippi River
- to Swiss Valley Park

WISC. | ILL.

N

HERITAGE TRAIL - Dubuque County

Deep rugged woodlands, sheer limestone bluffs, wetland communities and primitive prairies are just a few great reasons thousands of visitors each year enjoy the 26-mile Heritage Trail. Named for its rich cultural and natural heritage, the trail also offers farmland and wooded blufftop scenery, plus old mining and mill town remnants, as it follows the former Chicago Northwestern railbed from Dyersville to Dubuque.

The local hospitality is another highlight of this unique trail. In Dyersville, the Chamber of Commerce can arrange for visitors to stay in local homes. Graf serves the trailway with a comfortable campground and shower facilities, located right next to the trail.

Upon reaching Dubuque, visitors can enjoy its many recreational opportunities: greyhound racing, horseback riding, houseboat rental, art galleries and festivals. Dubuque features another enjoyable trail, the Floodwall Trail, which starts at 16th Street. For more tourist information, contact the Dyersville Area Chamber of Commerce, 143 1st Ave. West, P.O. Box 187, Dyersville, Iowa 52040, (319)875-2311; or the Dubuque Convention & Visitors Bureau, 770 Town Clock Plaza, Dubuque, Iowa 52001, (319) 557-9200 or 1-800-255-2255, ext.9200.

DYERSVILLE
Trailhead off Hwy. 136: parking*, restrooms, trail passes
City facilities
Bed & breakfast
Bike shop/repair
Camping
City parks
Golf course
Groceries
Hospital
Hotels/motels
Information center
Restaurants
Swimming pool

FARLEY
Trailhead at county road Y13: parking*, trail passes/maps/information

City facilities
Groceries
Lodging
Restaurants

KIDDER
Trailhead on Gun Club Road: parking, trail passes/maps/information

GRAF
Trailhead on Graf Road: parking*, restrooms, picnic tables, trail passes/maps/information
City facilities
Camping
City park
Convenience store
Restaurant
Showers

TWIN SPRINGS
Trailhead on Asbury Road: parking*, trail passes/maps/information

DURANGO
Trailhead at Hwy. 52 North & Burton Furnace Road: parking*, restrooms, drinking water, trail passes/maps/information
City facilities
Bed & breakfast
Restaurants

DUBUQUE
Trailhead at Rupp Hollow Rd. & Hwys. 52S/3W: parking*, restrooms, trail passes/maps/information, trail interpretive center
City facilities
Bed & breakfasts
Bike shop/repair
Camping
City parks
Groceries
Hotels/motels
Hospitals
Information center
Interpretive area
Public showers
Restaurants

*Handicap-accessible

HOURS: Open year-round, sunrise to sunset. **FEE:** $1.10/day or $5.25/year for ages 12-64; $.60/day or $2.75/year for 65 and over.
TRAIL FACTS: Total miles: 26; **Surfacing:** Crushed limestone; **Restrictions:** Snowmobiling allowed from Dubuque to Durango and from Twin Springs to Dyersville. Cross-country skiing is permitted from Dubuque to Graf.
INFORMATION: Swiss Valley Nature Center, 13768 Swiss Valley Road, Peosta, Iowa 52068; (319) 556-6745

HOOVER NATURE TRAIL 18

EMERGENCY
Dial 911
Morning Sun (319) 643-2121

Cedar Rapids — Ely — Solon — Morse — Oasis Trailhead — West Branch Trailhead — West Liberty — Nichols — Conesville Trailhead — Cranston — Columbus Junction — Wapello — Morning Sun Trailhead — Mediapolis — Sperry — Burlington — Muscatine — Y-Camp

Lake McBride State Park, Cedar River, Iowa River, Herbert Hoover National Historic Site, Presidential Library Museum, Depot Restoration, Cone Lake, Lake Odessa, 7 Ponds Recreational Area, Mississippi River, Skunk River

Segment distances: 6, 6, 2.5, 3.5, 8, 8, 7, 15, 6, 8, 7.5, 7, 3, 7

Highways: 1, 380, 218, 22, 92, 80, 6, 61, 92, 78, 61, 34

HOOVER NATURE TRAIL
- Linn, Cedar, Johnson, Muscatine, Louisa and Des Moines Counties

Historic Hoover Nature Trail is reminiscent of days gone by, with tiny towns, abandoned depot junctions and prairie remnants weaving their way around the old Rock Island Railway. In addition to prairies, heavily timbered areas line the trail and, in a few places, the trailway hugs a wooded bluff along the Iowa River. West Branch is the home of our 31st president and trail namesake, Herbert Hoover, and the town celebrates his birthright with a presidential library, museum and historic site.

Many creeks and lakes parallel or cross the trail, adding an abundance of wildlife to the scenery. Fox, deer, beaver and other animals and birds have been observed and appreciated on the trail. East of Conesville, it will access scenic Cone Lake, where trail users will be able to enjoy the park and camp.

Upon its completion, the Hoover Nature Trail will become Iowa's longest single recreational trail, spanning 15 towns and six counties. Currently, much of the trail remains under development, and portions of the trail marked here with dashes are private property yet to be purchased. Although visitors are encouraged to experience the completed segments and take in delightful southeast Iowa, public use of privately owned areas is not allowed. Prior to planning a trip on the Hoover Nature Trail, please call (319) 627-4250 for an update on trail development.

OASIS
Trailhead on Oasis Road: parking, restroom

WEST BRANCH
Trailhead at Beranek Park southeast of town: parking*, restrooms* (under construction)
City facilities
Bed and breakfast
Camping
City park
Groceries
Information center
Lodging
Medical clinic
Parking
Restaurants
Trail Passes

NICHOLS
Trailhead at City Park: parking*, picnic tables
City facilities
Bed and breakfast
City park
Convenience store
Restaurant

CONESVILLE
Trailhead at Shellabarger Park: parking*, shelter
City facilities
Convenience store
Restaurants
Trail passes

MORNING SUN
Trailhead on Division Street: parking*
City facilities
Convenience store
Restaurant

*Handicap-accessible

HOURS: Open year-round, no restrictive hours. **FEE:** User fee required: $1.00/day or $5.00/year.
TRAIL FACTS: Total miles: 115; **Miles completed:** 12 (Oasis to West Branch: 3.5 miles; Nichols to Conesville: 7 miles; Morning Sun: 1.5 miles north}; **Surfacing:** Crushed limestone; **Restrictions:** Equestrians must follow the marked path (West Branch to Oasis) or remain parallel to, but separate from, the limestone surface.
INFORMATION: Hoover Nature Trail, Box 123, West Liberty, Iowa 52776; (319) 627-2626 or (319) 627-4250

JACKSON COUNTY RECREATION TRAIL

EMERGENCY
Jackson County Sheriff
(319) 652-3312

JACKSON COUNTY RECREATION TRAIL - Jackson County

The Jackson County Recreation Trail traverses the banks of the Maquoketa River near Spragueville, offering breathtaking views of scenic bluffs. The natural beauty of this trail is derived from the river and limestone bluffs that border the abandoned Milwaukee Railroad railbed. Scenic overlooks along the trail provide striking views of this eastern Iowa river valley.

Visitors to this 3.7-mile trail benefit from the abundant natural attractions of the area surrounding the trail. The three communities of Bellevue, Sabula and Maquoketa are within a short distance of the trail and form a triangle-shaped area packed with local parks, wildlife areas, preserves and historical landmarks.

The Maquoketa Caves State Park offers caves to explore and rugged hiking trails that provide spectacular views of geological formations. In Bellevue State Park attractions along hiking trails include a butterfly garden, a historic mill, a quarry, and Woodland Culture Indian burial mounds. The nearby Green Island Wildlife Management Area provides marsh and timberland for wildlife habitat and public use. South Sabula Lakes Park is an ideal spot for those seeking water sports, and Spruce Creek county park features boating and camping.

Those interested in historical sites can see the Hurstville Lime Kilns and limestone architecture at the Big Mill Homestead near Bellevue. History and art are combined in Costello's Old Mill Gallery, an art gallery located in a nineteenth-century mill in Maquoketa.

For more information on the area, visitors can contact the Jackson County Welcome Center, R.R. #1, Box 1, Sabula, Iowa 52070, (800) 342-1837; or the Jackson County Conservation Board listed below.

SPRAGUEVILLE

Trailhead 1/4 mile east of Spragueville on 45th Street: parking*
Trailhead 4 miles north of Preston on County Road Z34: parking*
City facilities
City parks
County park with canoe access
Restaurant

*Handicap-accessible

HOURS: Open year-round, 6:00 a.m.-10:00 p.m.
FEE: No user fee required.
TRAIL FACTS: Total miles: 3.7; **Surfacing:** Crushed limestone; **Restrictions:** Hunting is not allowed on the trail.
INFORMATION: Jackson County Conservation Board, Courthouse, Maquoketa, Iowa 52060; (319) 652-3783

KEWASH NATURE TRAIL 20

EMERGENCY Dial 911

- TRAILHEAD — WASHINGTON pop. 7,074
- Conger House
- TRAILHEAD — WEST CHESTER pop. 191
- TRAILHEAD — KEOTA pop. 1,034

Roads: W55, W47, W19, W38, G36, G26, G32, V15, W15, 1, 92, 77

Trail segments: 6, 7

N

KEWASH NATURE TRAIL - Washington County

Delightful Kewash Trail traverses rich woodland areas and native prairie openings, providing a scenic tour of Iowa's southern valleys. From Keota to West Chester, the prairie is particularly resplendent, showing off such species as silver sage, rattlesnake master, gentian and blazing star. The West Chester to Washington segment is known for its beautiful woodlands and diverse wildlife species. Just past West Chester on Clemens Creek bridge, a panoramic view of a great valley woodland and rustic farm scenery enchants trail visitors. West of Washington, at Hayes Timber, giant red oaks dominate the forest with their widespread branches.

The trail name comes from the first syllables in Keota and Washington. The Kewash Trail follows the same route as the first railroad connecting young prairie towns. The red-tailed hawk is the trail's emblem, symbolizing our connection to the prairie that once flourished in Iowa.

For information on nearby tourist attractions, contact the Washington Chamber of Commerce, 212 N. Iowa Avenue, Washington, Iowa 52353; (319) 653-3272.

David Thoreson

KEOTA
Trailhead at city park: parking, restrooms, picnic tables, drinking water,
City facilities
Groceries
Restaurants

WEST CHESTER
Trailhead along trail: parking, restrooms, picnic tables, drinking water
City facilities
Convenience store

WASHINGTON
Trailhead at Sunset Park off W. Main: parking*, restrooms*, picnic tables, drinking water
City facilities
Bicycle shop/repair
Camping
Convenience store
Hospital
Lodging
Restaurants

*Handicap-accessible

HOURS: Open year-round, 4:30 a.m.-10:30 p.m.
FEE: User fee required for visitors over 16 years: $1.00/day, $5.00/year; available on trail.
TRAIL FACTS: Total miles: 13.8; **Surfacing:** Crushed limestone
INFORMATION: Washington County Conservation Board, 2939 Hwy. 92, Ainsworth, Iowa 52201; (319) 653-7765

LINN CREEK GREENBELT PARKWAY 21

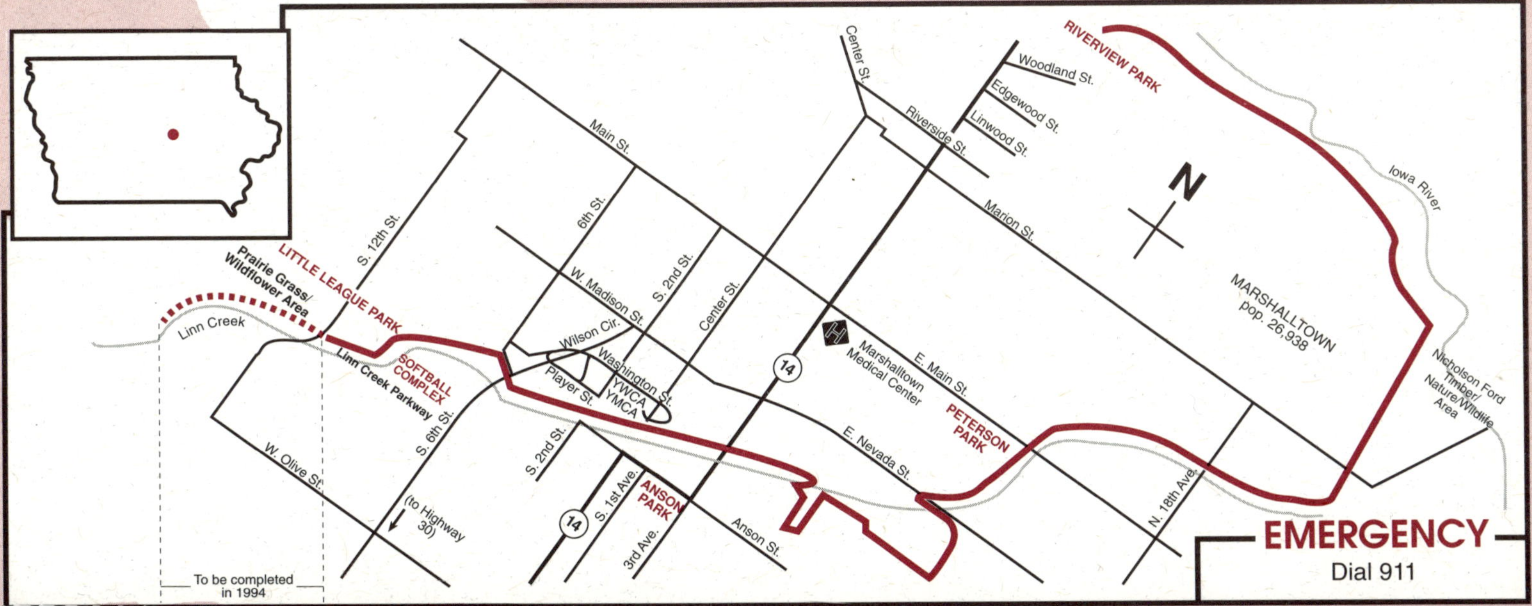

EMERGENCY Dial 911

MARSHALLTOWN pop. 26,938

- Nicholson Ford Timber/Wildlife Area
- Iowa River
- RIVERVIEW PARK
- Woodland St.
- Edgewood St.
- Linwood St.
- Riverside St.
- Marion St.
- S. 12th St.
- 6th St.
- S. 2nd St.
- Center St.
- W. Madison St.
- Wilson Cir.
- Washington St.
- YWCA/YMCA
- Player St.
- Main St.
- E. Main St.
- Marshalltown Medical Center
- PETERSON PARK
- E. Nevada St.
- N. 18th Ave.
- Anson St.
- 3rd Ave.
- ANSON PARK
- N. 1st Ave.
- S. 2nd St.
- S. 6th St.
- LITTLE LEAGUE PARK
- SOFTBALL COMPLEX
- Linn Creek Parkway
- Prairie Grass/Wildflower Area
- Linn Creek
- W. Olive St.
- (to Highway 30)
- To be completed in 1994

14

LINN CREEK GREENBELT PARKWAY - Marshalltown

The Linn Creek Greenbelt Parkway is a six-mile trail built on the dike that runs along Linn Creek and the Iowa River. It links several Marshalltown park and recreation areas that provide a variety of outdoor diversions. Not only do the parks offer options for picnicking along the way, but several feature playing fields for team sports. At Riverview Park visitors can camp and use the swimming pool.

While city parks line the trail, unique natural attractions can also be found along the way. The Nicholson Ford Nature Area features scenic views of river bottom timberland and marsh. Trail users can observe prairie grasses and wildflowers at the prairie area near the west end of the trail.

In addition to recreational opportunities, Marshalltown offers many historical and cultural attractions. For tourism information contact the Marshalltown Convention and Visitors Bureau, 709 South Center, Marshalltown, Iowa 50158, (515) 753-6645; or the Marshalltown Parks and Recreation Department listed below.

MARSHALLTOWN
City facilities
Bike shop/repair/rental
Camping
City park
County park
Golf courses
Groceries
Hospital
Lodging
Public showers
Restaurants
State parks
Swimming pools

RIVERVIEW PARK
Trailhead is at Highway 14 north and Woodland Street.
Camping
Drinking water
Parking
Phones (at pool)
Picnic tables
Restrooms
Shelter
Swimming pool

PETERSON PARK
Trailhead is at 15th and Woodbury.
Parking
Picnic tables

ANSON PARK
Trailhead is at 3rd Avenue and Anson Street.
Drinking water, Parking*
Picnic tables
Restrooms*
Shelter

SOFTBALL COMPLEX
Trailhead is at South 6th Street along Linn Creek.
Concessions
Drinking water
Parking*
Phones
Picnic tables
Restrooms*
Shelter

LITTLE LEAGUE PARK
Trailhead is at 12th Street along Linn Creek.
Concessions
Drinking water
Parking*
Restrooms

*Handicap-accessible

HOURS: Open year-round, 6:00 a.m.-11:30 p.m.   **FEE:** No user fee required.
TRAIL FACTS: Total miles: 8; **Miles completed:** 6; **Surfacing:** Asphalt;
Restrictions: Snowmobiling adjacent to trail along bottom of dike. No hunting allowed.
INFORMATION: Marshalltown Parks & Recreation Department, 803 North 3rd Avenue, Marshalltown, Iowa 50158; (515) 754-5715

ORANGE CITY/ALTON PUDDLE JUMPER TRAIL 22

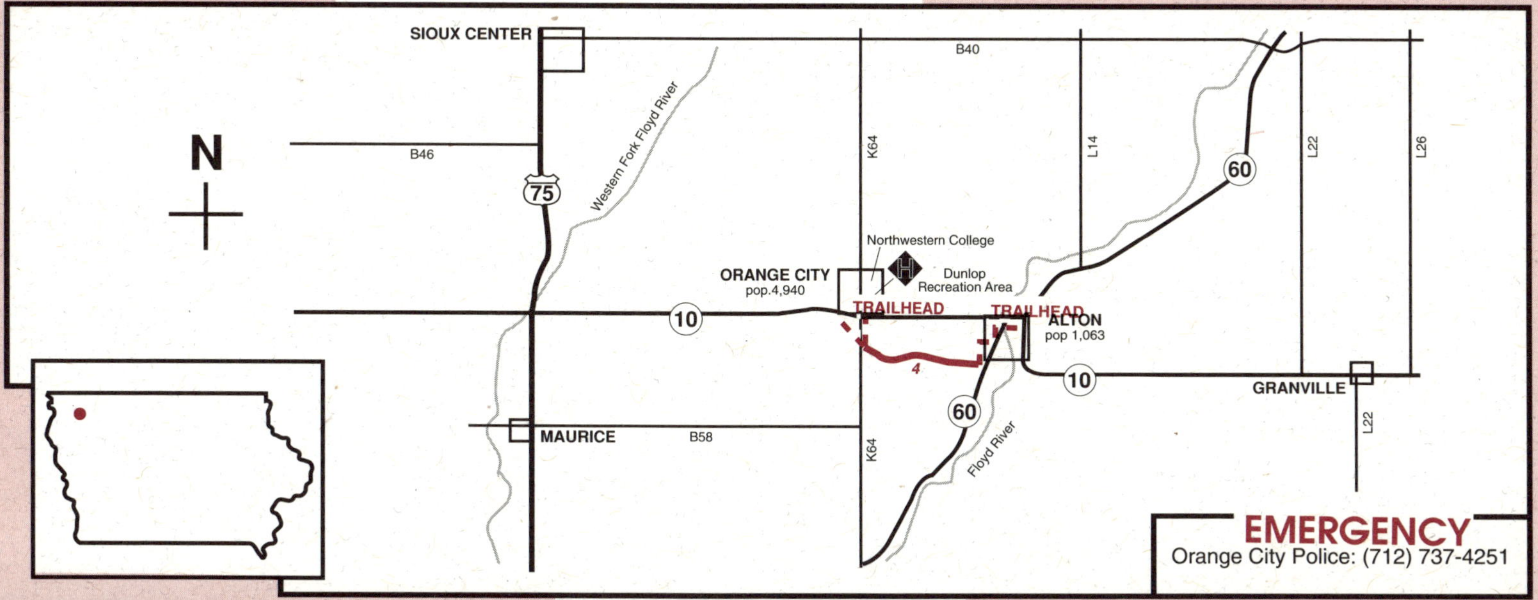

EMERGENCY
Orange City Police: (712) 737-4251

- GRANVILLE
- ALTON pop. 1,063
- ORANGE CITY pop. 4,940
- MAURICE
- SIOUX CENTER
- Northwestern College
- Dunlop Recreation Area
- Floyd River
- Western Fork Floyd River
- TRAILHEAD
- TRAILHEAD

Roads: L22, L26, L14, B40, B46, B58, K64, 10, 60, 75

N

ORANGE CITY/ALTON PUDDLE JUMPER TRAIL - Sioux County

Lying in the heart of the Floyd River valley and the midwestern plains, this northwestern trail provides some truly unique scenery. Bison roam the fenced property adjacent to the trail. (Please stay on the trail side of the fence, and don't feed the animals.) Two small lookout towers enable trail visitors to properly view these amazing animals, so remember your binoculars! Adding to the scenery are native prairie flowers and grasses planted by science professors from local Northwestern College.

The Puddle Jumper Trail joins the two quaint towns of Orange City and Alton, and trail visitors will enjoy the rural town friendliness of local citizens. You won't want to miss the Orange City Tulip Festival in May.

Tourist information may be obtained by contacting the Orange City Chamber of Commerce, 125 Central Ave. SE, Orange City, Iowa 51041; (712) 737-4510.

Ty Smedes

ORANGE CITY
Trailhead at County Road K64: parking, picnic tables
City facilities
Bike shop/repair
Camping
Groceries
Hospital
Lodging
Restaurants

ALTON
Trailhead in middle of trail, on gravel road off Hwy. 10: parking*, restrooms, picnic tables, drinking water, shelter
Trailhead just west of Alton on gravel road off Hwy. 10: parking, picnic tables
City facilities
Camping
Groceries
Restaurants

*Handicap-accessible

HOURS: Open year-round, no restrictive hours.
FEE: No user fee required.
TRAIL FACTS: Total miles: 2.3; **Surfacing:** Crushed quartzite
INFORMATION: Mel at City Hall, 125 Central Avenue SE, Orange City, Iowa 51041; (712) 737-4885

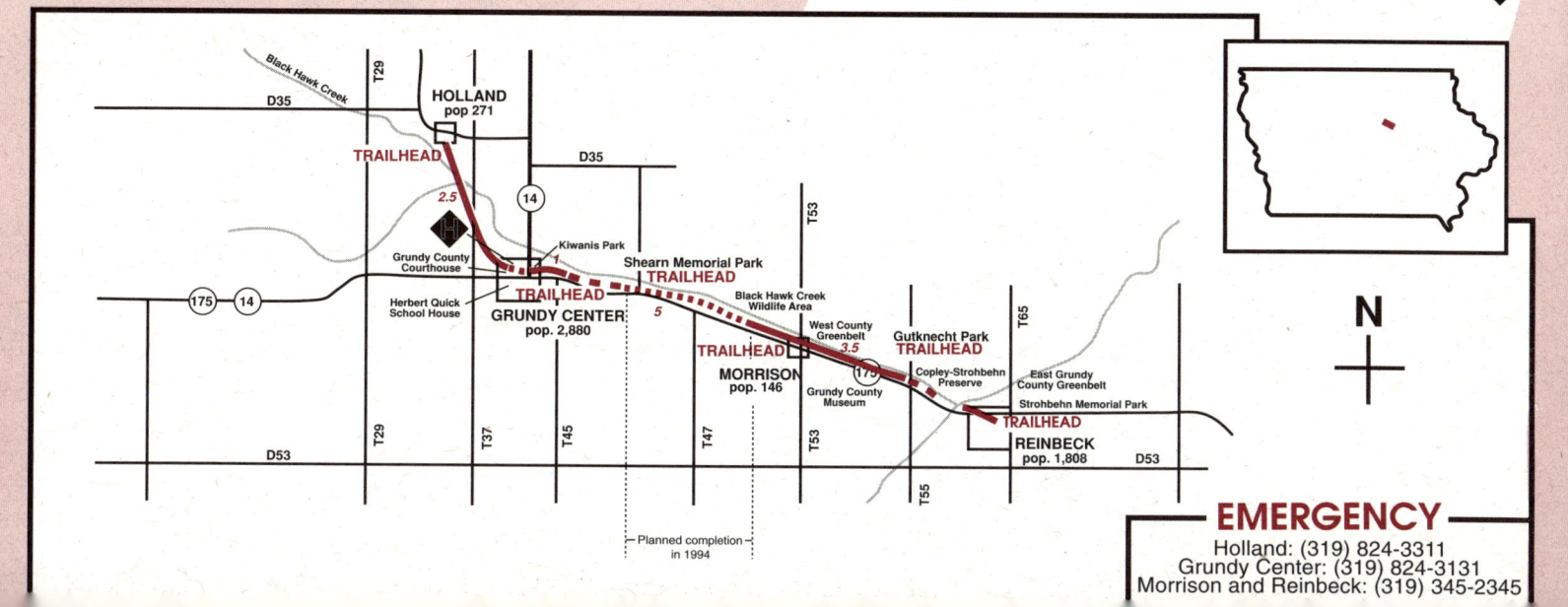

PIONEER TRAIL 23

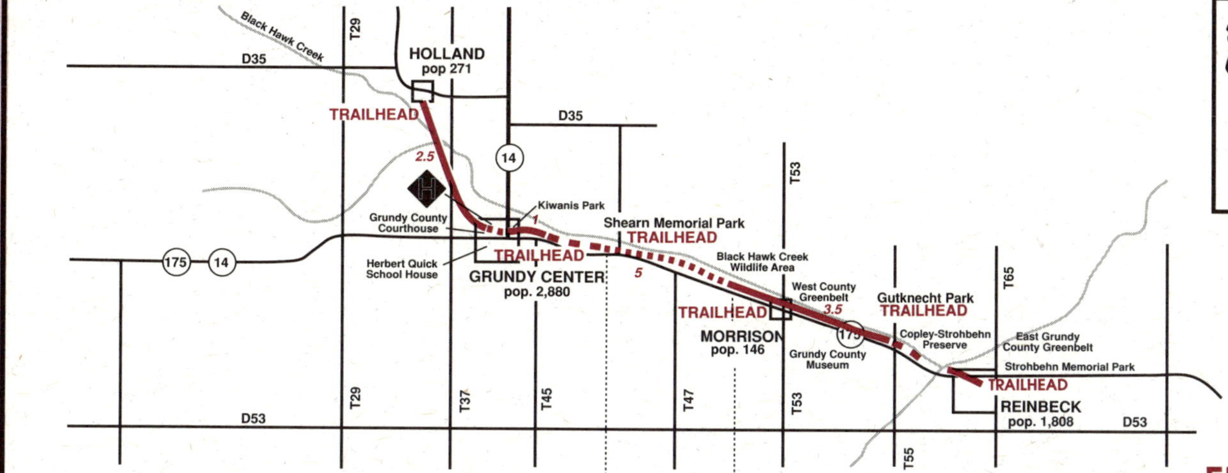

EMERGENCY
Holland: (319) 824-3311
Grundy Center: (319) 824-3131
Morrison and Reinbeck: (319) 345-2345

REINBECK pop. 1,808
MORRISON pop. 146
GRUNDY CENTER pop. 2,880
HOLLAND pop 271

TRAILHEAD (Reinbeck)
TRAILHEAD (Gutknecht Park / Copley-Strohbehn)
TRAILHEAD (Morrison)
TRAILHEAD (Grundy Center / Shearn Memorial Park)
TRAILHEAD (Holland)

Strohbehn Memorial Park
East Grundy County Greenbelt
Copley-Strohbehn County Preserve
Gutknecht Park
Grundy County Museum
West County Greenbelt 3.5
Black Hawk Creek Wildlife Area
Shearn Memorial Park
Kiwanis Park
Herbert Quick School House
Grundy County Courthouse
Black Hawk Creek

Planned completion in 1994

5
2.5

T65, T55, T53, T47, T45, T37, T29
D53, D35
175, 14

PIONEER TRAIL - Grundy County

Named in recognition of pioneers who settled Grundy County in the 1850s, the Pioneer Trail is another example of Iowa's rich heritage. Interspersed throughout the trail are four segments of the Grundy County Greenbelt, providing necessary coverage for a variety of animal and bird life, as well as native prairie vegetation which has remained virtually intact over the years due to its proximity to the railbed. The Black Hawk Creek Wildlife Area, a quarter mile journey north of Morrison on County T-53, offers visitors two self-guided nature trails with over 100 labeled plants and a swinging suspension bridge.

The Grundy County Museum, located in Morrison, gives visitors a taste of our past with natural and human history interpretive exhibits. The museum also includes an 1853 log cabin (the first building ever constructed in Grundy County), a restored 1870 country school house, and railroad history.

There is currently no public access to the half-mile gaps in the trail just east of Grundy Center and just west of Reinbeck.

Tourist information may be obtained by contacting the Grundy Center Chamber of Commerce, 705 F Avenue, Grundy Center, Iowa 50638; (319) 824-3838.

HOLLAND
Trailhead south of County Road D-35 in Holland: parking, equestrian parking
City facilities
City park
Groceries
Restaurant

GRUNDY CENTER
Trailhead at Kiwanis Park off N. 2nd Street: parking, restrooms
Trailhead on A Avenue: parking
City facilities
Bike shop/repair
City park
Groceries
Hospital
Lodging
Restaurants

SHEARN PARK
Trailhead is at Hwy. 175 & County Road T47.
Drinking water
Parking*
Picnic tables
Restrooms*
Shelter

MORRISON
Trailhead at Railroad St. one block north of Hwy. 175: parking
City facilities
City park
Picnic tables (at museum)
Restaurants

GUTKNECHT PARK
Trailhead is at Hwy. 175 & County Road T55.
Camping
Drinking water
Equestrian parking
Parking*
Picnic tables
Restrooms*
Shelter

REINBECK
Trailhead at Grundy County Greenbelt off N. Commercial Street: parking, equestrian parking, restrooms, picnic tables, camping.
City facilities
City park
Groceries
Medical clinic
Restaurants

*Handicap-accessible

HOURS: Open-year round, sunrise to sunset. **FEE:** No user fee required.
TRAIL FACTS: Total miles: 12; **Miles completed:** 7;
Surfacing: Crushed limestone with parallel grass surface for equestrian use
INFORMATION: Grundy County Conservation Board, Box 36, Morrison, Iowa 50657; (319) 345-2688

PRAIRIE FARMER RECREATIONAL TRAIL 24

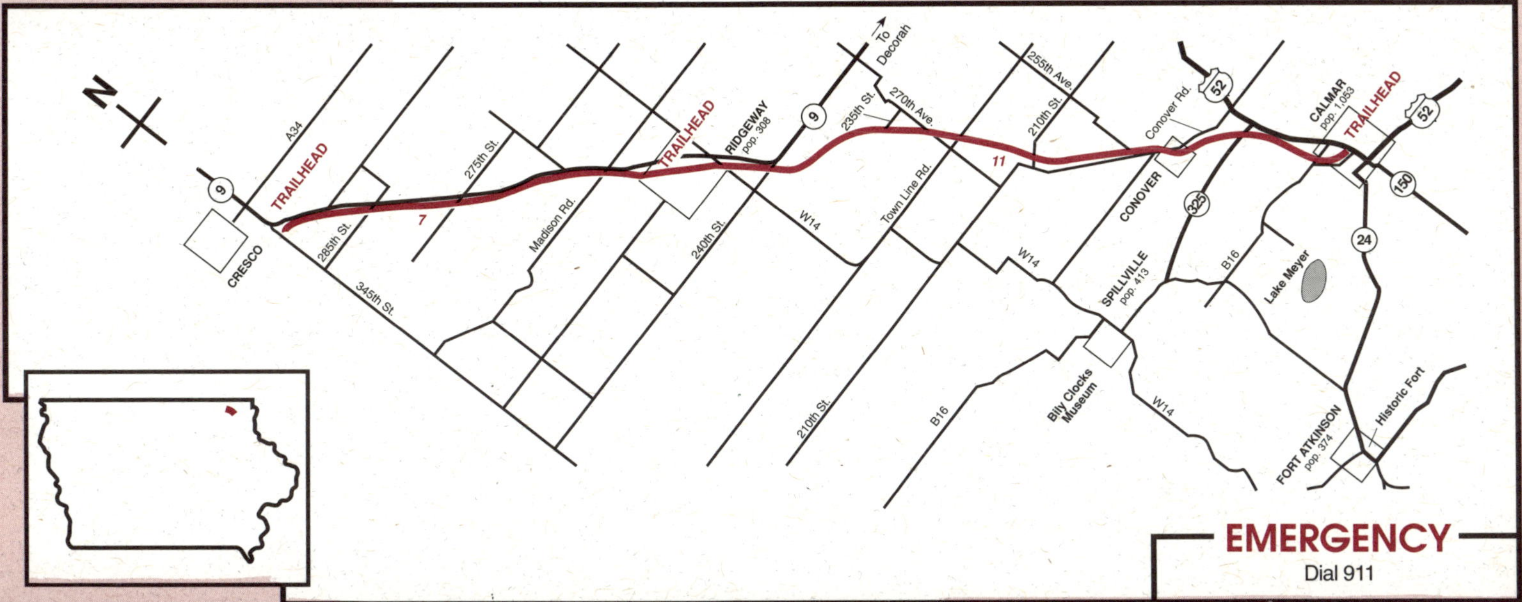

EMERGENCY Dial 911

PRAIRIE FARMER RECREATIONAL TRAIL- Winneshiek County

Named for an old radio show once broadcast in the Midwest, the Prairie Farmer Recreational Trail follows the abandoned Milwaukee Railroad line from Calmar to near Cresco. As with other railroad corridors, much of this route is lined with native prairie areas that have remained undisturbed. As a result, the 18-mile Prairie Farmer trail runs through sections of prairie that contain rare native plant species. It also offers segments of woodland scenery for variety.

Visitors may want to begin their journey at the Old Depot in Calmar. The depot, which is currently being renovated, serves as a trailhead and a tourism information center. At Ridgeway, the trail follows city streets. The trail ends two miles east of Cresco.

Area towns near the trail feature a variety of museums, historical attractions and parks. At Fort Atkinson, visitors can see the 1840s fort, grounds and museum. The Vesterheim Norwegian-American Museum, which is located in Decorah, features exhibits on immigrant life from old Norway to pioneer America.

For those seeking outdoor adventure, nearby parks include Lake Meyer Park: 160 acres of picnicking, camping, boating and nature study opportunities. Chimney Rock Park, near Bluffton, and Kendallville Park offer canoe access to the famous bluffs and limestone cliffs of the picturesque Upper Iowa River.

Trail users may want to plan visits around local festivals. Calmar celebrates its annual Farmers Day in June, and Decorah hosts Nordic Fest in July.

Tourism information can be obtained from Winneshiek County Tourism/Decorah Chamber of Commerce, 102 East Water Street, Decorah, Iowa 52101, (319) 382-3990; or Calmar Tourism/City Clerk, 112 North Maryville, Calmar, Iowa 52132, (319) 562-3154.

CALMAR
Trailhead at the Old Depot, Railroad and Highway 52: parking*
City facilities
Bed & breakfasts
Bike shop/repair/rental
Camping
City park
Groceries
Information center
Medical clinic
Restaurant
State park
Swimming pool

RIDGEWAY
Trailhead at Ridgeway Park: parking*, restrooms, picnic tables, drinking water, shelter
City facilities
City parks
Convenience store
County park
Restaurant

CRESCO
Trailhead 2 miles east of Cresco: parking
City facilities
City park
Groceries
Hospital
Information center
Lodging
Restaurant

*Handicap-accessible

HOURS: Open year-round, 6:00 a.m.-10:30 p.m. **FEE:** No user fee required.
TRAIL FACTS: Total miles: 18; **Surfacing:** Crushed limestone; **Restrictions**: Snowmobiling only allowed on the section from Ridgeway to Cresco. Hunting is allowed on some sections; check with the Winneshiek County Conservation Board for more detailed information.
INFORMATION: Winneshiek County Conservation Board, 2546 Lake Meyer Road, Fort Atkinson, Iowa 52144: (319) 534-7145

RACCOON RIVER VALLEY TRAIL

EMERGENCY Dial 911

Towns and Features

- **STUART** — I-80
- **DESOTO** — Hwy 169
- **ADEL** (pop. 2,846) — TRAILHEAD, Adel Historical Museum, Kuehn Conservation Area
- **REDFIELD** (pop. 959) — TRAILHEAD, Redfield Depot, Hanging Rock Geological Formation, Nation's Bridge Park
- **OTTRVILLE** — TRAILHEAD, Wagon Bridge, French Castle Courthouse, Brick Streets
- **WAUKEE** (pop. 2,296) — TRAILHEAD
- **DALLAS CENTER**
- **LINDEN** (pop. 264) — TRAILHEAD
- **PANORA** (pop. 1,211) — TRAILHEAD, Lenon Mill Park, Michael Mills City Park, Lake Panorama, Turn of the Century Museum, Panora Depot
- **YALE** (pop. 299) — TRAILHEAD, Lake Panorama National Golf Course
- **GUTHRIE CENTER** — TRAILHEAD

Rivers
- Raccoon River
- Middle Raccoon River
- North Raccoon River
- South Raccoon River

Highways/Roads
35, 80, 6, 9, 10, 44, 25, 169, F90, F64, F59, F51, R16, R22, P48, P28, P58, P46, P30, P18, F25, F32, F63, N70, 925

N (compass)

RACCOON RIVER VALLEY TRAIL - Dallas and Guthrie Counties

The Raccoon River Valley Trail offers 34 scenic miles that wind through the Raccoon River Greenbelt. The prairie remnants and bottomland timber areas are reminiscent of early Iowa when the Chicago Northwestern railroad was constructed. Trees line much of the asphalt trail, sometimes creating a tunnel or canopy effect.

Patches of native prairie wildflowers and grasses are found throughout the trail. Because of its diverse ecosystems, the trail serves as wildlife habitat for a variety of species.

The Classic Bike Festival, held in May, promotes antique, classic and unique bikes. Other community festivals include Redfield's Old Settlers Day in early June, the Yale Fourth of July Celebration, Panorama Days and the Adel Sweetcorn Festival held in August, and the Waukee Fall Festival in September. For more tourist information, contact the Adel Chamber of Commerce, P.O. Box 214, Adel, Iowa 50003, (515) 993-4525; or the Panora Chamber of Commerce, P.O Box 73, Panora, Iowa 50216; (515) 755-3300.

WAUKEE
Trailhead at Hwy. 6 and County Road R22: parking*, restrooms*, trail passes
City facilities
City parks
Groceries
Restaurants

ORTONVILLE
Trailhead at Hwy. 6 and County Road R16: parking*, trail passes

ADEL
Trailhead on 18th Street: parking*, restrooms*, trail passes

City facilities
Bike shop/repair/rental
Camping
City parks
Groceries
Restaurant

REDFIELD
Trailhead at old train depot, north of Hwy. 6: parking*, restrooms*, trail passes, concessions, railroad exhibit
City facilities
Groceries
City park
Restaurant

LINDEN
Trailhead at County Rd. P30 & city park: parking*, restrooms, drinking water, trail passes
City facilities
City parks

PANORA
Trailhead on Hwy. 44: parking*, picnic tables, drinking water, trail passes/maps/information, restaurant
City facilities
Bike shop/repair/rental
Camping
City park
Groceries
Medical clinic
Restaurants
Trail passes

Lake Panorama Resort has restaurant, lodging and golf course

YALE
Trailhead at SE edge of town on County Road F25: parking*, restrooms, picnic tables, drinking water, trail passes/maps/information
City facilities
City park
Groceries
Trail passes

*Handicap-accessible

HOURS: Open year-round, 6:00 a.m. to sundown. **FEE:** User fee required (18 and over): $1.00/day or $6.00/year.
TRAIL FACTS: Total miles: 34; **Surfacing:** Asphalt; **Restrictions:** Hunting and snowmobiling (minimum of 4 inches of snow) allowed only in Guthrie County.
INFORMATION: Dallas County Conservation Department, 1477 K Avenue, Perry, Iowa 50220; (515) 465-3577 or Guthrie County Conservation Board, RR 2, Box 4A17, Panora, Iowa 50216; (515) 755-3061

RIVER CITY GREENBELT AND TRAIL SYSTEM 26

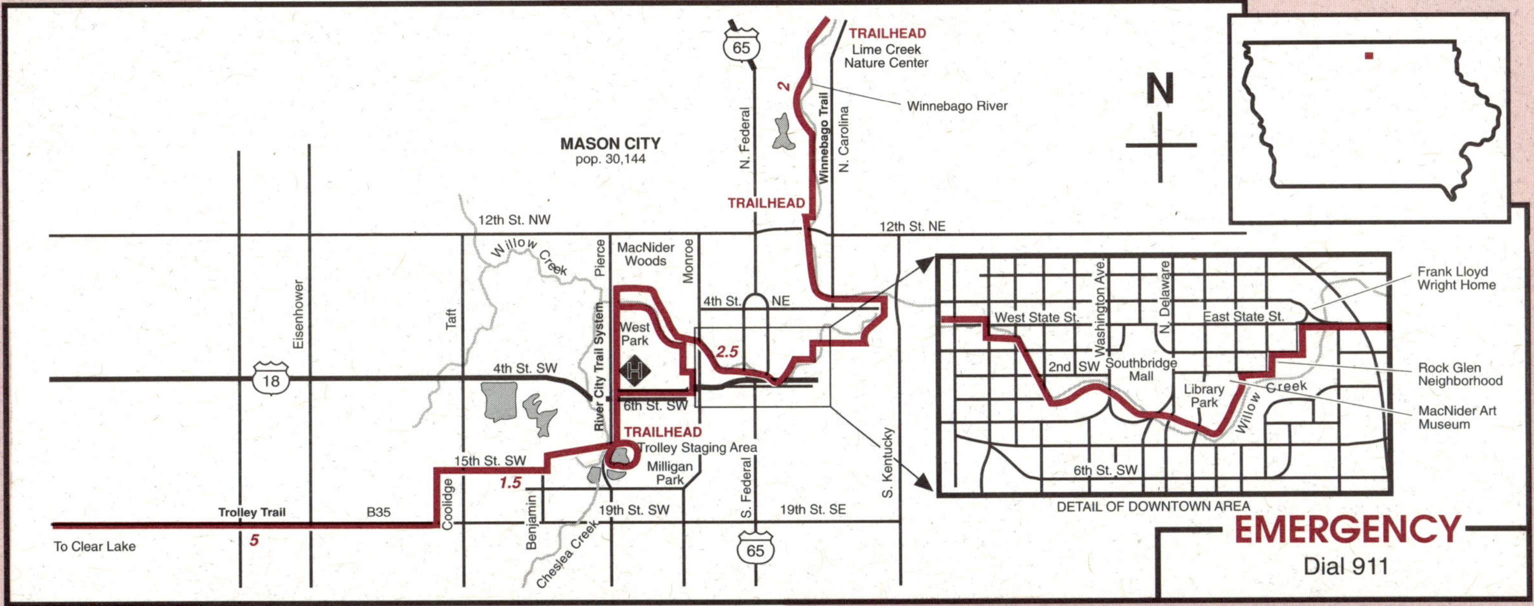

EMERGENCY Dial 911

DETAIL OF DOWNTOWN AREA

- MacNider Art Museum
- Rock Glen Neighborhood
- Frank Lloyd Wright Home
- Library Park
- Willow Creek
- Southbridge Mall
- 6th St. SW
- 2nd SW
- Washington Ave.
- N. Delaware
- East State St.
- West State St.
- S. Kentucky

MASON CITY pop. 30,144

- To Clear Lake
- Trolley Trail
- Coolidge
- B35
- 19th St. SW
- 15th St. SW
- 19th St. SE
- S. Federal
- Benjamin
- Chelsea Creek
- Milligan Park
- Trolley Staging Area
- River City Trail System
- 6th St. SW
- 4th St. SW
- 4th St. NE
- Monroe
- Pierce
- Taft
- Eisenhower
- MacNider Woods
- West Park
- Willow Creek
- 12th St. NW
- 12th St. NE
- N. Carolina
- N. Federal
- Winnebago Trail
- Winnebago River
- Little Creek Nature Center

TRAILHEAD (×3)

65, 18, 5

1.5, 2.5, 2

N

RIVER CITY GREENBELT AND TRAIL SYSTEM
- Cerro Gordo County

The diverse and far-reaching River City Greenbelt & Trail System offers something for everyone. It consists of three trails: the Trolley Trail, which connects Mason City and Clear Lake; the River City Trail, which links the parks and cultural attractions of Mason City; and the Winnebago Trail, which leads to the Lime Creek Nature Center.

The Trolley Trail runs parallel to a county road and Mason City's electric trolley line. Trail users are able to see America's last working electric trolley as it operates between Mason City and Clear Lake.

The River City Trail connects outlying Milligan and East Parks with downtown areas. The trail follows along an abandoned railroad bed, woods, parks and city streets. Scenic views of Willow Creek, the Winnebago River and Big Blue Lake also add interest to the trail. A special downtown walking tour uses interpretive plaques to identify attractions, such as the Meredith Willson Footbridge, the MacNider Art Museum and a Frank Lloyd Wright home.

The Winnebago Trail follows the Winnebago River to the Lime Creek Nature Center, traversing meadow and woods and offering picturesque views of the limestone bluffs along the river. At the nature center, visitors can see exhibits, use the observation deck or hike the four-mile trail system.

For more information on the Mason City/Clear Lake area, contact the Mason City Convention & Visitors Bureau, P.O. Box 1128, Mason City, Iowa 50401, (515) 423-5724; or the Clear Lake Convention & Visitors Bureau, 205 Main Ave., Clear Lake, Iowa 50428, (515) 357-2159.

MASON CITY
Trailhead at Milligan Park: parking*, restrooms*, picnic tables
Trailhead at Elm and 13th Street: parking, picnic tables
Trailhead at Lime Creek Nature Center: parking, restrooms, drinking water, picnic tables, interpretive area
City facilities
Bike shop/repair
Camping
Groceries
Hospitals
Lodging
Nature center
Public showers
Restaurants

CLEAR LAKE
City facilities
Bike shop/repair
Camping
City parks
Groceries
Information center
Lodging
Medical clinic
Public showers
Restaurants

*Handicap-accessible

HOURS: Open year-round, 6:00 a.m.-11:00 p.m.   **FEE:** No user fee required.
TRAIL FACTS: Total miles: 15.5 (Trolley Trail: 5 miles; River City Trail: 8.5 miles; Winnebago Trail: 2 miles);   **Surfacing:** The Trolley trail is asphalt; the Winnebago Trail is crushed limestone; and the River City Trail incorporates sections of paved trail, crushed limestone and city streets.
INFORMATION: Mason City Parks & Recreation Department, 22 North Georgia, Mohawk Square, Mason City, Iowa 50401; (515) 421-3673

SAC AND FOX TRAIL 27

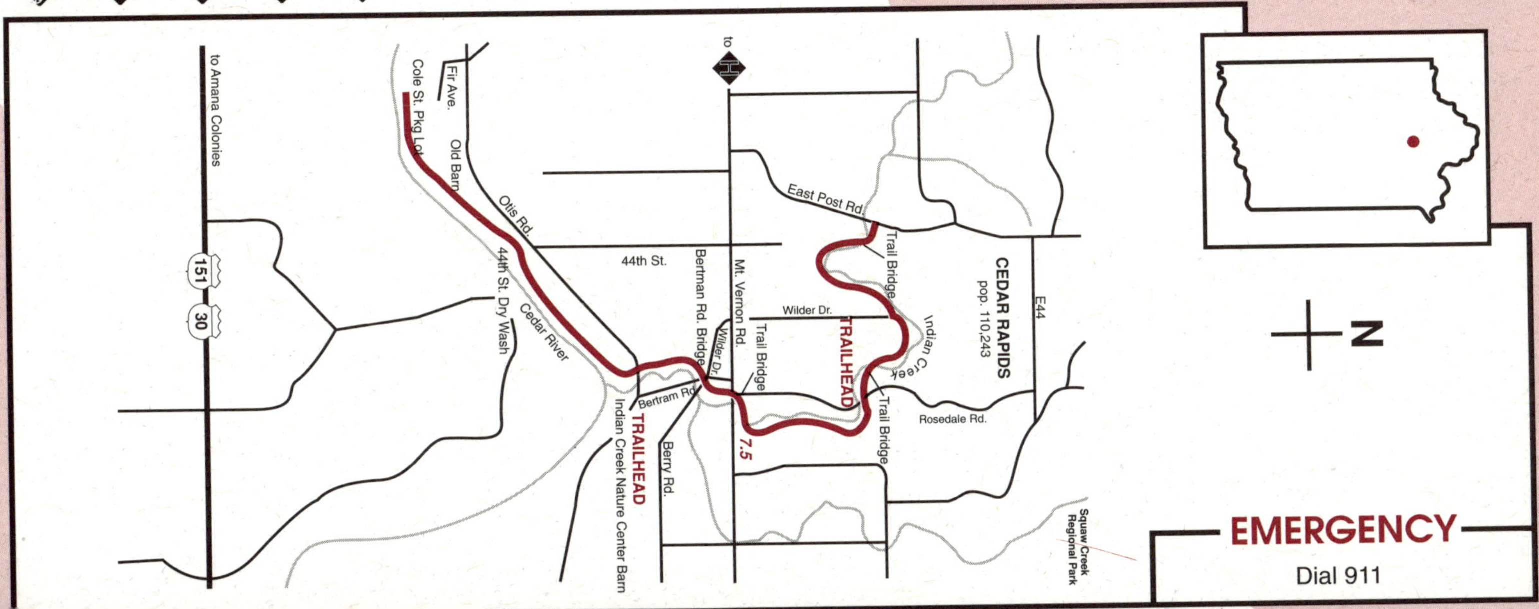

EMERGENCY Dial 911

CEDAR RAPIDS
pop. 110,243

- Squaw Creek Regional Park
- Rosedale Rd.
- Trail Bridge
- Indian Creek
- E44
- Trail Bridge
- East Post Rd.
- Wilder Dr.
- Mt. Vernon Rd.
- Trail Bridge
- 7.5
- TRAILHEAD
- Berry Rd.
- Bertram Rd.
- TRAILHEAD
- Indian Creek Nature Center Barn
- Bertram Rd. Bridge
- 44th St.
- Cedar River
- 44th St. Dry Wash
- Otis Rd.
- Fir Ave.
- Old Barn
- Cole St. Pkg Lot
- US 30
- 151
- to Amana Colonies

N

SAC AND FOX TRAIL - Cedar Rapids

Named for the American Indians banished from Illinois to Iowa, the Sac and Fox Trail is Iowa's first National Recreation Trail. Approximately one-half of the trail winds through a deep forest valley, created by scenic Indian Creek. The remaining trail, with more open terrain, follows the Cedar River. Adjoining the Sac and Fox trail in a series of loops is the narrow and winding Cedar Greenbelt Trail, unsuitable for horses and bicycles, but exciting on foot!

In addition to the trail's beauty and diversity, the Indian Creek Nature Center adds an educational twist to this historical area. Trail users can visit the center's exhibits and gift shop. A naturalist is also available to answer questions.

Visitors may want to plan a trip around the Maple Syrup Festival, held the first weekend in March, or the Trail Festival, held on the Sunday closest to Columbus Day. For more information on the Cedar Rapids area, contact the Cedar Rapids Convention & Visitors Bureau, 119 1st Avenue SE, Cedar Rapids, Iowa; (319) 398-5009.

Roger A. Hill

INDIAN CREEK NATURE CENTER
Trailheads at Otis, Bertram and Rosedale Roads have parking. (There is foot access at East Post Road, Mt. Vernon Road and Cole Street.)
Drinking water
Exhibits
Gift shop
Maps
Naturalist
Restrooms
Telephone

CEDAR RAPIDS
City facilities
Bed & breakfasts
Bike shop/repair
City parks
Camping
Groceries
Hospitals
Lodging
Restaurants

HOURS: Open year-round, 6:00 a.m.-10:00 p.m.
FEE: No user fee required.
TRAIL FACTS: Total miles: 7.5;   **Surfacing:** Crushed limestone
INFORMATION: Cedar Rapids Parks Department, City Hall, Cedar Rapids, Iowa 52401; (319) 398-5080

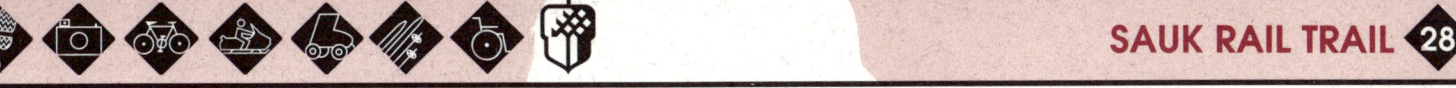

SAUK RAIL TRAIL 28

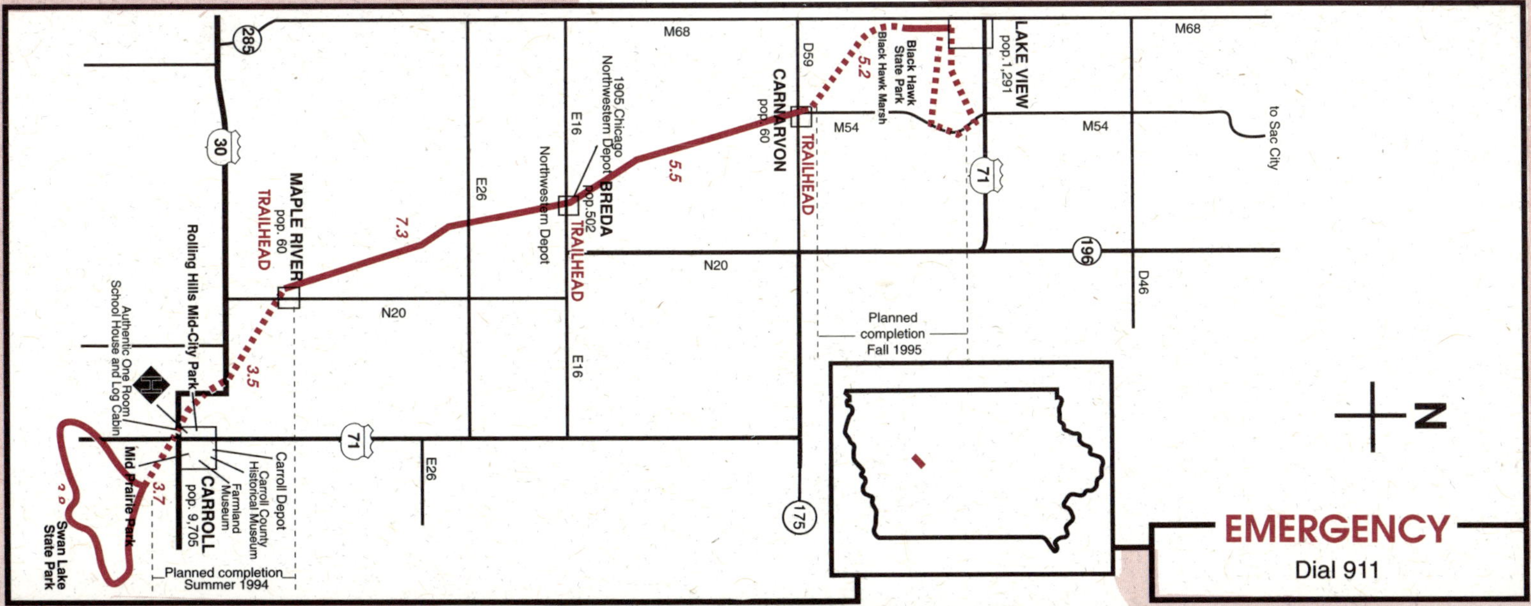

EMERGENCY Dial 911

N

To Sac City

LAKE VIEW pop. 1,291
Black Hawk State Park
Black Hawk Marsh

CARNARVON pop. 60
TRAILHEAD

BREDA pop. 502
1905 Chicago Northwestern Depot
Northwestern Depot
TRAILHEAD

MAPLE RIVER pop. 60
TRAILHEAD

CARROLL pop. 9,705
Carroll Depot
Carroll County Historical Museum
Farmland Museum
Planned completion Summer 1994
Mid Prairie Park
Swan Lake State Park
Authentic One Room School House and Log Cabin
Rolling Hills Mid-City Park

Planned completion Fall 1995

5.2
5.5
7.3
3.5
3.7

175 · 71 · 30 · 285 · 196

D46 · D59 · M54 · M68 · N20 · E16 · E26

SAUK RAIL TRAIL - Carroll and Sac Counties

This multi-purpose trail, named for the Sac Indian tribe that spent summers in Carroll County, is being developed with a targeted completion date of late 1994. Upon its completion, you'll experience 33 miles of natural prairies, wetlands, rich farmland and timber areas, plus an abundance of wildlife. The former Chicago Northwestern railbed will begin and end at two beautiful state parks, both of which are home to lakes offering a multitude of recreational activities. The 13-mile midsection of the trail from Maple River to Carnarvon follows a valley floor — you'll travel through the Hazelbrush Wildlife Area, an 80-acre county park full of native flora and fauna. Historic railroad depots and several quality antique shops may be found in the towns of Breda and Carroll. The completed trail portion includes 3.8 miles around Swan Lake and 13 miles from Maple River to Carnarvon.

Upon its completion, the Sauk Rail Trail will truly prove to be an exciting trip! For more tourism information, contact the Carroll Chamber of Commerce, 223 West Fifth, Carroll, Iowa 51401, (712) 792-4383; or Sac County Economic and Tourism Development, 615 Main, Sac City 50583, (712) 662-7383.

LAKE VIEW
Trailhead to be determined.
City facilities
Bed & breakfast
Camping
City park
Hotel/motels
Groceries
Public showers
Medical clinic
Restaurants

CARNARVON
Trailhead on east edge of County Road D54: parking
City facilities
Restaurant

BREDA
Trailhead at Breda City Park: parking*, equestrian parking, restrooms*, picnic tables, phone, drinking water, trail passes/maps/information, concessions
City facilities
City park
Groceries
Public showers
Restaurants

MAPLE RIVER
Trailhead at county blacktop N20: parking*, equestrian parking, trail passes/maps/information,
City facilities
Restaurant

CARROLL
Trailhead to be determined.
City facilities
Bike shop/repair
City park
Groceries
Hospital
Information center
Lodging
Public showers
Restaurants

SWAN LAKE
Trailhead is inside park area.
Bike rental
Boating
Camping
Concessions
Drinking water
Maps
Parking*
Picnic tables
Restrooms*
Shelter
Showers

*Handicap-accessible

HOURS: Open year-round 5:00 a.m.-10:30 p.m. **FEE:** User fee required for ages 12 and over (Maple River to Carnarvon only): $1.00/day or $5.00/year.
TRAIL FACTS: Total miles: 33 planned; **Miles completed:** 16.8 (Swan Lake: 3.8 miles; Maple River to Carnarvon: 13 miles); **Surfacing:** Blacktop; limestone from Maple River to Carnarvon; **Restrictions:** Equestrian use allowed adjacent to trail. Hunting is allowed on some sections.
INFORMATION: Carroll County Conservation Board, RR 1 Box 240A, Carroll, Iowa 51401; (712) 792-4614 or Sac County Conservation Board, 2970 280th Street, Sac City, Iowa 50583; (712) 662-4530

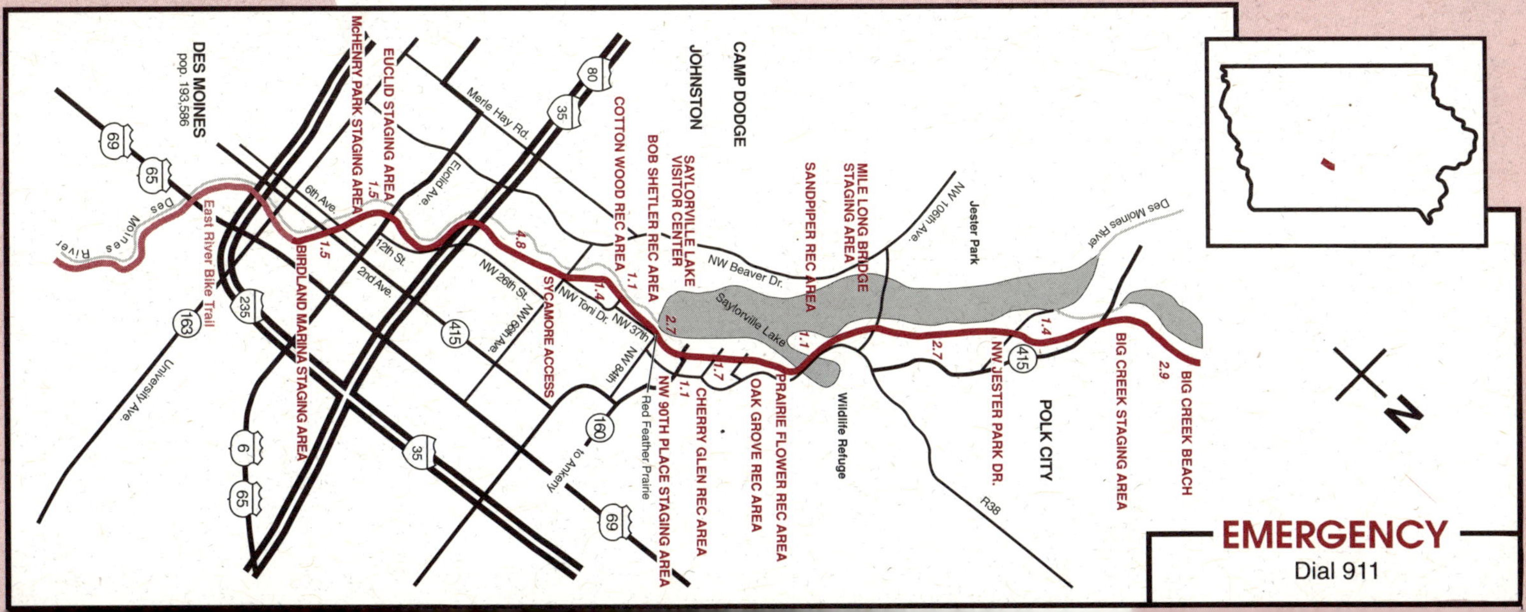

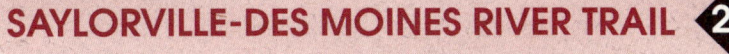

SAYLORVILLE-DES MOINES RIVER TRAIL

EMERGENCY Dial 911

- BIG CREEK BEACH
- BIG CREEK STAGING AREA
- NW JESTER PARK DR.
- PRAIRIE FLOWER REC AREA
- OAK GROVE REC AREA
- CHERRY GLEN REC AREA
- NW 90TH PLACE STAGING AREA
- MILE LONG BRIDGE STAGING AREA
- SANDPIPER REC AREA
- SAYLORVILLE LAKE VISITOR CENTER
- BOB SHETLER REC AREA
- COTTON WOOD REC AREA
- SYCAMORE ACCESS
- BIRDLAND MARINA STAGING AREA
- EUCLID STAGING AREA
- McHENRY PARK STAGING AREA

POLK CITY
Wildlife Refuge
Saylorville Lake
Jester Park
Des Moines River
NW 106th Ave.
NW Beaver Dr.
Red Feather Prairie
to Ankeny
CAMP DODGE
JOHNSTON
Merle Hay Rd.
Euclid Ave.
NW 66th Ave.
NW 26th St.
NW York Dr.
NW 5th
NW 84th
2nd Ave.
12th St.
9th Ave.
University Ave.
East River Bike Trail
Des Moines River

DES MOINES
pop. 193,586

Distances: 2.9, 1.4, 2.7, 1.1, 1.7, 1.1, 2.7, 1.1, 1.4, 4.8, 1.5, 1.5

DES MOINES

Birdland Marina Staging Area
- Concessions
- Drinking water
- Marina
- Parking
- Phones
- Picnic tables
- Restrooms

McHenry Park Staging Area
- Drinking water
- Lodging
- Parking*
- Phones
- Picnic tables
- Restrooms*

Euclid Staging Area
- Parking

JOHNSTON

Bob Shetler Recreation Area Trailhead at NW 78th Avenue.
- Camping
- Drinking water
- Parking*
- Phones
- Picnic tables
- Restrooms*

Sycamore Access Trailhead at NW 66th Avenue.
- Boat ramp
- Parking*

Cottonwood Recreation Area Trailhead at NW 37th Street & NW Toni Drive.
- Drinking water
- Fishing pier
- Parking
- Phone
- Picnic tables
- Playground
- Restrooms*
- Shelter

ANKENY

NW 90th Place Staging Area
- Parking

Cherry Glen Recreation Area Trailhead at NW 94th Avenue.
- Boat ramp
- Camping
- Drinking water
- Parking*
- Phone
- Picnic tables
- Restrooms*
- Shelter

Oak Grove Recreation Area Trailhead at NW 98th Avenue.
- Beach
- Drinking water
- Parking*
- Phone
- Picnic tables
- Playground
- Restrooms*
- Shelter

Saylorville Lake Visitor Center: Trailhead at NW Horseshoe Road.
- Drinking water
- Interpretive exhibits
- Nature trail
- Parking*
- Phone
- Restrooms*
- Trail maps/information

POLK CITY

Prairie Flower Recreation Area Trailhead at NW Lake Drive.
- Camping
- Drinking water
- Parking*
- Phone
- Playground
- Restrooms*
- Shelter

Sandpiper Recreation Area Trailhead at NW McBride Drive.
- Beach
- Boat Ramp
- Drinking water
- Groceries
- Parking*
- Phone
- Picnic tables
- Playground
- Restrooms*
- Shelter

Mile Long Bridge Staging Area Trailhead at NW 112th.
- Convenience store
- Parking

NW Jester Park Drive
- Fishing access
- Parking at Big Creek Spillway

Big Creek Staging Area Trailhead at NW Madrid Drive.
- Beach
- Boat ramp/rental
- Concessions
- Drinking water
- Parking*
- Phone
- Picnic tables
- Restrooms*
- Shelter
- Trail maps/information

Big Creek Beach
- Beach
- Boat ramp
- Drinking water
- Parking
- Phone
- Picnic tables
- Restrooms
- Shelter

*Handicap-accessible

HOURS: Open year-round, 6:00 a.m.-10:00 p.m.
FEE: No user fee required.
TRAIL FACTS: Total miles: 23.7; **Surfacing:** Asphalt
INFORMATION: U.S. Army Corps of Engineers, 5600 NW 78th Avenue, Johnston, Iowa 50131; (515) 276-4656 or (515) 964-0672

SAYLORVILLE-DES MOINES RIVER TRAIL - Polk County

The result of many years of planning and cooperation between the City of Des Moines, the Iowa Department of Natural Resources and the U.S. Army Corps of Engineers, this trail offers a variety of terrain, beautiful scenery and colorful vegetation. Rugged hills and picturesque valleys are found in the upper segments and observant visitors will see deer, squirrels, wood ducks, song birds and other wildlife species.

At Saylorville, enjoy the fragrance of mock orange, honeysuckle and wildflowers along the trail, which is dominated by a view of the expansive lake. The trail traverses a range of landscapes including bottomland, shaded forest, oak uplands and meadows. Rustling cornfields and rolling valleys are sprinkled with picnic areas and sparkling beaches, providing plenty of pit stops along the way!

The 170-acre reconstructed Red Feather Prairie, with savannas, woodlands and bottomland, includes 11 grass species and 38 flower species which bloom throughout the warmer months.

Adjacent to the Arboretum, near the Visitor Center, is a small prairie and several bridges. A garden to be added to this area will provide habitat and wind protection for butterflies. Upon its completion, the butterfly garden will be one of the largest butterfly areas in the state, offering a colorful display of perennials and annuals.

Unusual tree species along the trail also provide botanical beauty. The Big Creek area is scattered with Chinkapin Oaks, which naturally grow in limestone outcroppings. A large stand of Kentucky Coffee trees, recognizable by the thick pods that hang from the branches, inhabit the area north of Cottonwood. The tree was named by settlers who roasted its seeds for a coffee substitute.

The Saylorville-Des Moines River trail continues on to the south as the East River Bike trail that winds through the Des Moines metro area. Bikers should note that the only bike rental available in the area is Polk City Bike Rental near Sandpiper Recreation Area. (If the Iowa Natural Heritage Foundation is mentioned when renting a bike, helmet rental is free!)

The trail and adjacent recreation areas are used by thousands of people throughout the year. The variety of uses and diverse terrain offer recreational enjoyment for everyone! For more tourist information, contact the Des Moines Convention & Visitors Bureau, 309 Court Avenue, Des Moines, Iowa 50309; (515) 286-4960.

The Iowa Department of Transportation, through its Recreational Trails Program, has provided significant funding for construction of many of the trails featured in this guide. To learn how the DOT can assist trail and bikeway development near you, call (515) 239-1621, or write Iowa Department of Transportation, Recreational Trails Program, 800 Lincoln Way, Ames, IA 50010.

SHELL ROCK RIVER TRAIL 30

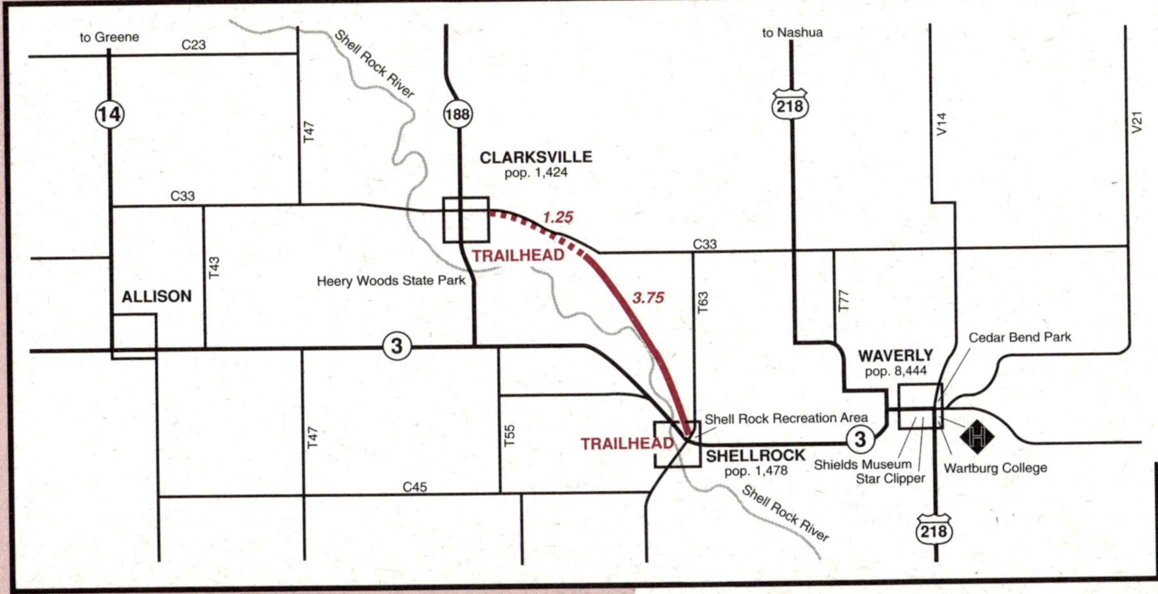

EMERGENCY

Clarksville Ambulance Service:
(319)278-4597
Shell Rock: Dial 911
Waverly: Dial 911

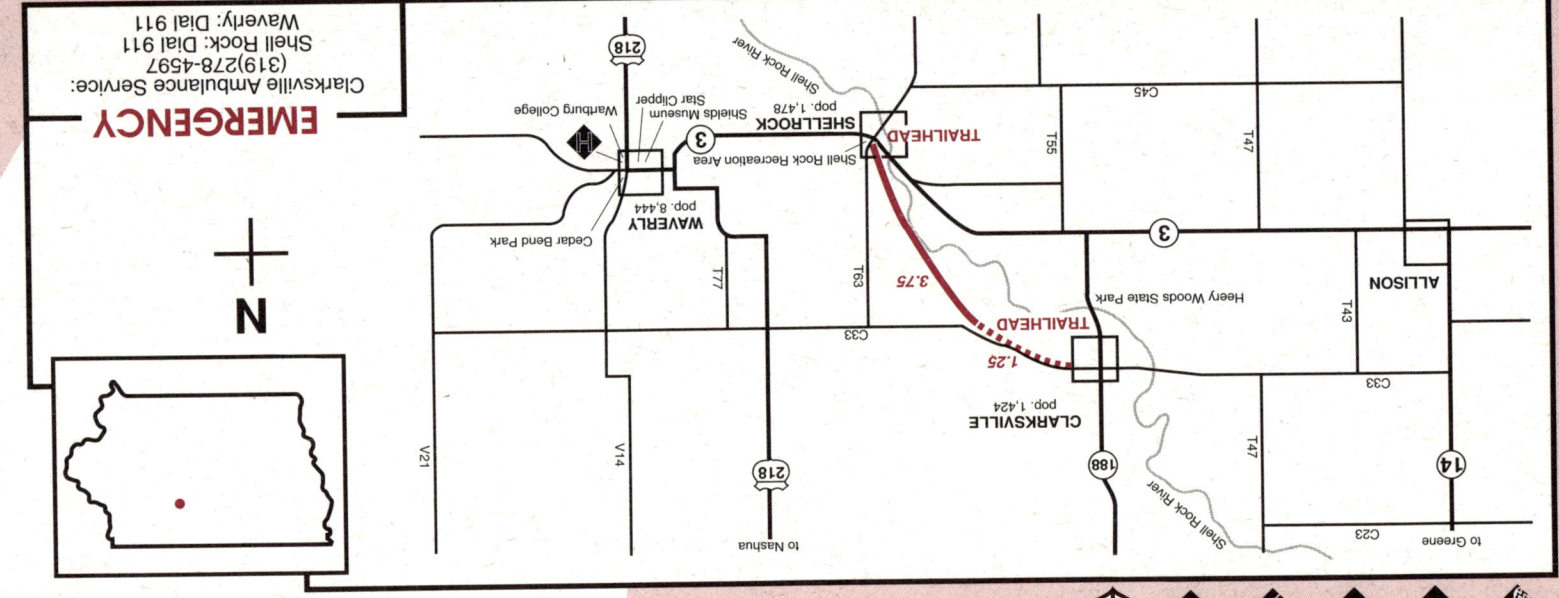

SHELL ROCK RIVER TRAIL - Butler County

Following the Shell Rock River valley, the former Chicago Northwestern route links the two rural Iowa towns of Clarksville and Shell Rock. The proximity of the towns to the Shell Rock and Cedar Rivers offers much opportunity to observe native flora and fauna while experiencing rural Iowa at its best. Much of the trail is lined with prairie grasses, and the surrounding area is abundant with animal wildlife.

Both towns possess a festive spirit. Lively street dances, fireworks, canoe floats and parades are all-time favorites in this area. Clarksville hosts Pioneer Days the first weekend in June. Shell Rock's locally famous Shell Rock Days begins July 3 and ends on the Fourth. In Greene, another nearby town just off Highway 14, festivities take place in mid-June during River Days. Allison hosts the Butler County Fair beginning the second Wednesday in July. Waverly boasts one of the world's largest horse sales held in March and October, and offers quaint downtown shopping and affordable lodging.

For more tourist information, please contact the Waverly Chamber of Commerce, 118 W. Bremer, Waverly, Iowa 50677, (319) 352-4526.

Bob Coyle

CLARKSVILLE
Trailhead 2 miles SE of Clarksville on gravel road (inquire locally for specific location): parking*
City facilities
Camping
City park
County park
Groceries
Restaurant

SHELL ROCK
Trailhead at Hwy. 3 and County Road T63: parking*
City facilities
Camping
City park
Convenience store
Restaurant

WAVERLY
City facilities
Bed & breakfast
Bike shop/repair
Camping
City park
Groceries
Hospital
Lodging
Restaurants

*Handicap-accessible

HOURS: Open year-round, sunrise to sunset.   **FEE:** No user fee required.
TRAIL FACTS: Total miles: 5;   **Miles completed:** 3.75 (The 1.25 mile northernmost segment needs limestone oversurfacing, but is accessible);
Surfacing: Crushed limestone
INFORMATION: Butler County Conservation Board, RR 1, Clarksville, Iowa 50619; (319) 278-4237

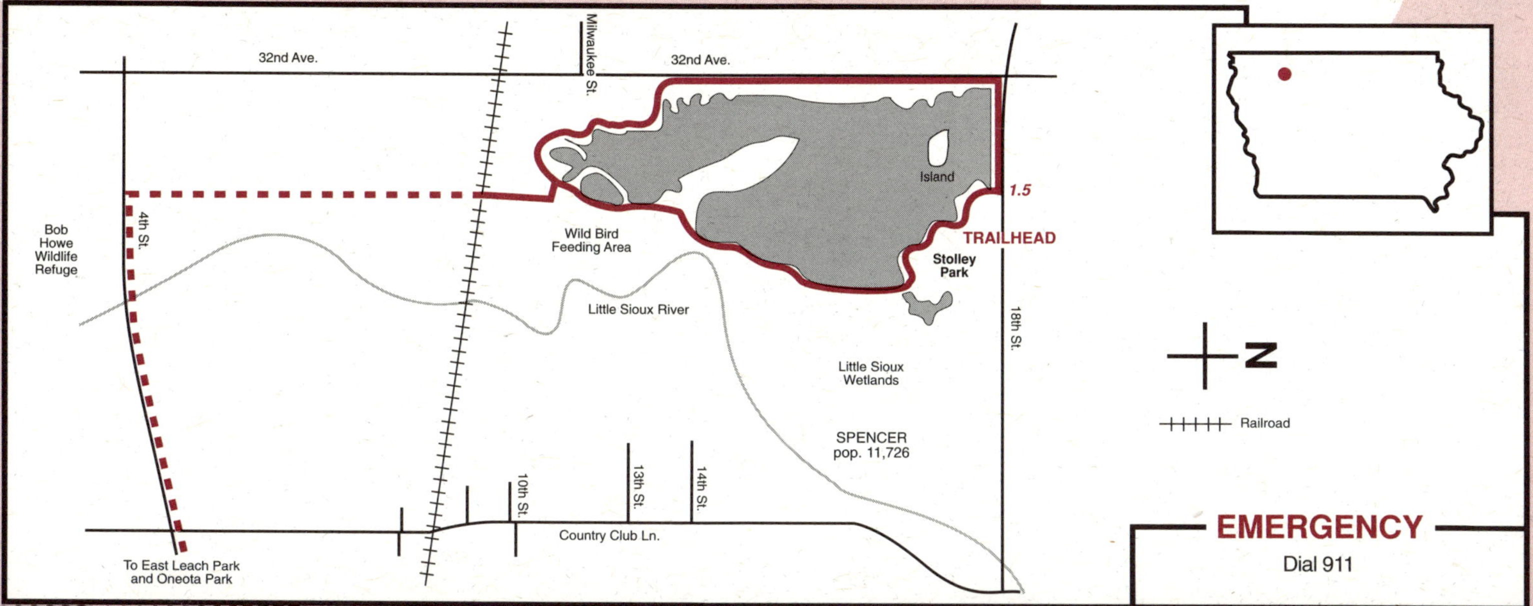

SPENCER RECREATIONAL TRAIL

EMERGENCY — Dial 911

N

+++++ Railroad

SPENCER pop. 11,726

- Country Club Ln.
- 14th St.
- 13th St.
- 10th St.
- 18th St.
- Little Sioux Wetlands
- Little Sioux River
- Stolley Park
- TRAILHEAD 1.5
- Island
- Wild Bird Feeding Area
- Milwaukee St.
- 32nd Ave.
- 4th St.
- Bob Howe Wildlife Refuge
- 32nd Ave.
- To East Leach Park and Oneota Park

31

SPENCER RECREATIONAL TRAIL - Spencer

The Spencer Recreational Trail travels through picturesque wooded lowlands around a pond in Spencer's Stolley Park and along the Little Sioux River. The trail lies adjacent to the Little Sioux Wetlands and near the Bob Howe Wildlife Refuge. The gently rolling landscape matches the relaxing atmosphere of the trail area. Benches are placed at strategic scenic locations, and signage along the trail interprets the abundant plant and animal life.

The Stolley Park area was once quarried for the sand and gravel left by the last glaciers to move across Iowa. Now the area is terraced for picnicking and recreation. Fishing and canoeing are permitted in the pond, but motorized boating is not allowed. Native plants can be found in special gardens and a feeding area encourages wild birds and game. Nesting boxes for Canada geese are situated on a small island in the pond, and the park features a pair of resident trumpeter swans. When the trail is completed it will connect Stolley Park with East Leach and Oneota parks.

For tourism information, contact the Spencer Area Association of Business and Industry, P.O. Box 3047, Spencer, Iowa 51301; (712) 262-5680.

Ty Smedes

SPENCER
Trailhead at Stolley Park:
parking*,
restrooms*,
drinking water,
picnic tables,
shelter
City facilities
Bed & breakfasts
Bike shop/repair
Camping
City parks
County parks
Golf courses
Groceries
Hospital
Hotels/motels
Information center
Public showers
Restaurants

*Handicap-accessible

HOURS: Open year-round, no restrictive hours.
FEE: No user fee required.
TRAIL FACTS: Total miles: 4.5 miles planned; **Miles completed:** 1.5; **Surfacing:** Crushed limestone and concrete
INFORMATION: Spencer Park Department, 418 2nd Avenue West, Spencer, Iowa 51301; (712) 264-7260

STORM LAKE LAKETRAIL

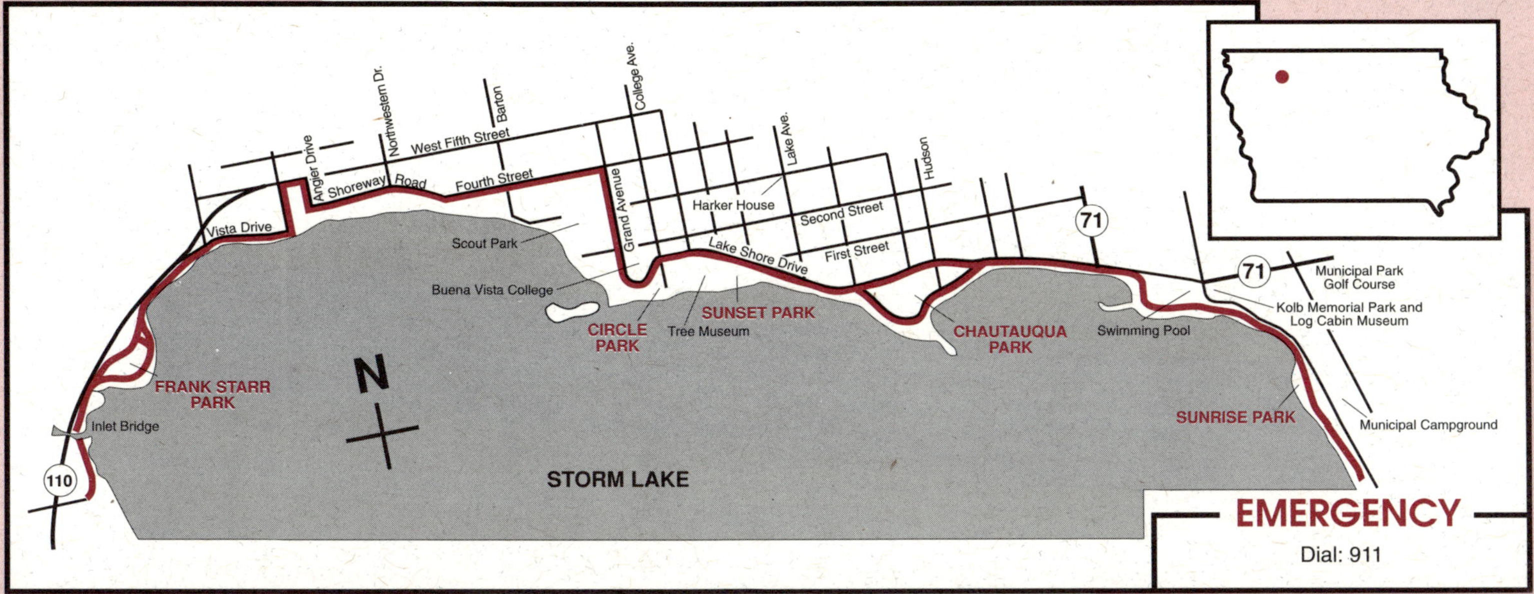

EMERGENCY

Dial: 911

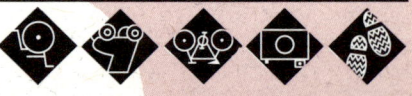

STORM LAKE LAKETRAIL - Storm Lake

The ideal combination of features from both city and recreational lake create the unique character of the Storm Lake LakeTrail. The five-mile trail links new pathways with existing sidewalks and low-traffic streets and runs through recreation, historic and residential areas.

As trail users move from park to park, they can be assured of an abundance of picnicking and outdoor activity, including water sports. Set sail from a boat ramp, swim on the beach, fish from a rock jetty or just enjoy a game of horseshoes. Beside the spectacular waterfront views along the north shore of the lake, there are numerous points of interest lining the trail, such as the Kolb Memorial Fountain and Garden and the Buena Vista College campus.

Of historic significance are the log cabin museum and the area of older, historic homes. The Harker House Museum, a few blocks from the trail, contains furniture and other items used by the original occupants, the family of an early Storm Lake banker. The Living Heritage Tree Museum offers history in an outdoor setting.

In addition to all of the activities and attractions of the trail, Storm Lake is host to the renowned Star Spangled Spectacular, a popular Fourth of July festival, and the Great Iowa Balloon Race held on Labor Day weekend.

For more visitor information, contact the Storm Lake Chamber of Commerce, 111 West 6th Street, Storm Lake, Iowa 50588; (712) 732-3780.

♿ Future plans provide for the addition of handicap-accessible parking and restrooms along the trail.

STORM LAKE
City facilities
Bed & breakfast
Bike shop/repair/rental
Camping
City park
Golf course
Groceries
Hospital
Hotels/motels
Information center
Public showers
Restaurants
Swimming pool

SUNRISE PARK
Parking
Picnic tables
Shelter

CHAUTAUQUA PARK
Parking
Picnic tables
Restrooms
Shelter

SUNSET PARK
Parking
Restrooms

CIRCLE PARK
Parking
Picnic tables
Primitive restrooms

SCOUT PARK
Parking
Playground
Restrooms

FRANK STARR PARK
Parking
Picnic tables
Restrooms
Shelters

HOURS: Open year-round, no restrictive hours. **FEE:** No user fee required.
TRAIL FACTS: Total miles: 5; **Surfacing:** Concrete with segments that fall directly on low-traffic city streets;
Restrictions: No hunting.
INFORMATION: Storm Lake Parks and Recreation Department, 620 Erie Street, Storm Lake, Iowa 50588; (712) 732-8027

THREE RIVERS TRAIL 33

EMERGENCY Dial 911

Trailheads and Locations

- **EAGLE GROVE** pop. 4,324 — TRAILHEAD, Historical Museum
- **THOR** pop. 200 — TRAILHEAD
- **DAKOTA CITY** pop. 1,072 — TRAILHEAD, Site of Fort Confederation Trading Post
- **HUMBOLT** pop. 4,794 — TRAILHEAD, Harry Reasoner's Boyhood Home, Humbolt County Historical Museum
- **GILMORE CITY** — TRAILHEAD
- **RUTLAND** pop. 163
- **BRADGATE** pop. 151 — TRAILHEAD
- **ROLFE** — TRAILHEAD, Historic site of the last American Indian battle
- **HARDY**
- **RENWICK**

Features

- Boone River
- Gotch State Park
- John Brown Park
- Wildcat Wonderland Playground
- Indian Creek
- Lizard Lake
- Union Cemetery
- Pioneer Cemetery
- West Fork Des Moines River
- Pilot Creek Wildlife Area
- Des Moines River East Fork

Roads

- 169 (to Fort Dodge)
- 3, 15, 17
- C49, C48, C44, P59, P92, P66, P63, P33, P20, P19, R62, C30, C26

Trail Segments (miles)

- 4.5, 3, 12, 4, 3, 10, 5

N

THREE RIVERS TRAIL - Pocahontas, Humboldt and Wright Counties

The Three Rivers Trail covers three counties and offers miles of uninterrupted woodlands, marshes, river valleys, and open prairie. With the addition of a section extending to Eagle Grove in 1994, the trail will cross the Boone River and the East and West forks of the Des Moines River in northwestern Iowa.

Unique to Three Rivers Trail is its rich American Indian and pioneer heritage. The Humboldt County Historic Museum and the Historic Museum in Eagle Grove will be accessible from the trail. Bradgate is the site of the last American Indian battle in Iowa, and a stagecoach route follows the trail between Bradgate and Rutland. Another special feature of Three Rivers Trail is its 36 railway bridges, all of which will remain intact and become a part of the trail. A detour east of Rolfe is planned for 1994. The trail will follow county roads until it is completed.

For tourism information, contact the Humboldt Chamber of Commerce, Municipal Bldg., 29 Fifth Street S., Humboldt, IA 50548; (515) 332-1481

ROLFE
Trailhead at Sunset Ridge Park: parking, restrooms, picnic tables, shelter, showers, fishing
City facilities
City park
Groceries
Restaurants

BRADGATE
Trailhead on King Street: parking, restrooms
City facilities
Convenience store
Restaurants

RUTLAND
Trailhead on Washington Avenue: parking, restrooms*, picnic tables, shelter
City facilities
Convenience store

PILOT CREEK WILDLIFE AREA
Parking*
Picnic tables
Trail interpretive area

HUMBOLDT
Trailheads at Hwy. 169 and Hwy. 3: parking
City facilities
Camping
City park
Groceries
Hospital
Lodging
Restaurants

GOTCH STATE PARK
Camping
Parking*
Picnic tables
Restrooms
Shelter
Water

DAKOTA CITY
Trailhead on 5th Avenue North: parking, restrooms*, picnic tables, shelter
City facilities
Convenience store
Restaurant

THOR
Trailhead on County Road P66: parking, restrooms, picnic tables, shelter
City facilities
Convenience store
Restaurant

EAGLE GROVE
Trailhead 3/4 mile west off 6th Street north: parking, restrooms, picnic tables, shelter
City facilities
Groceries
Lodging

*Handicap-accessible

HOURS: Open year-round, from sunrise to sunset.   **FEE:** No user fee required.
TRAIL FACTS: Total miles: 44;   **Miles completed:** 36.5 (Bradgate to west of the Boone River: 32; north and west of Gotch Park: 4.5));
Surfacing: Crushed limestone
INFORMATION: Humboldt County Conservation Board, Courthouse, Dakota City, IA 50529; (515) 332-4087 or Pocahontas County Conservation Board, R. R. 2, Box 11A, Pocahontas, IA 50574; (712) 335-4395

VOLKSWEG TRAIL 34

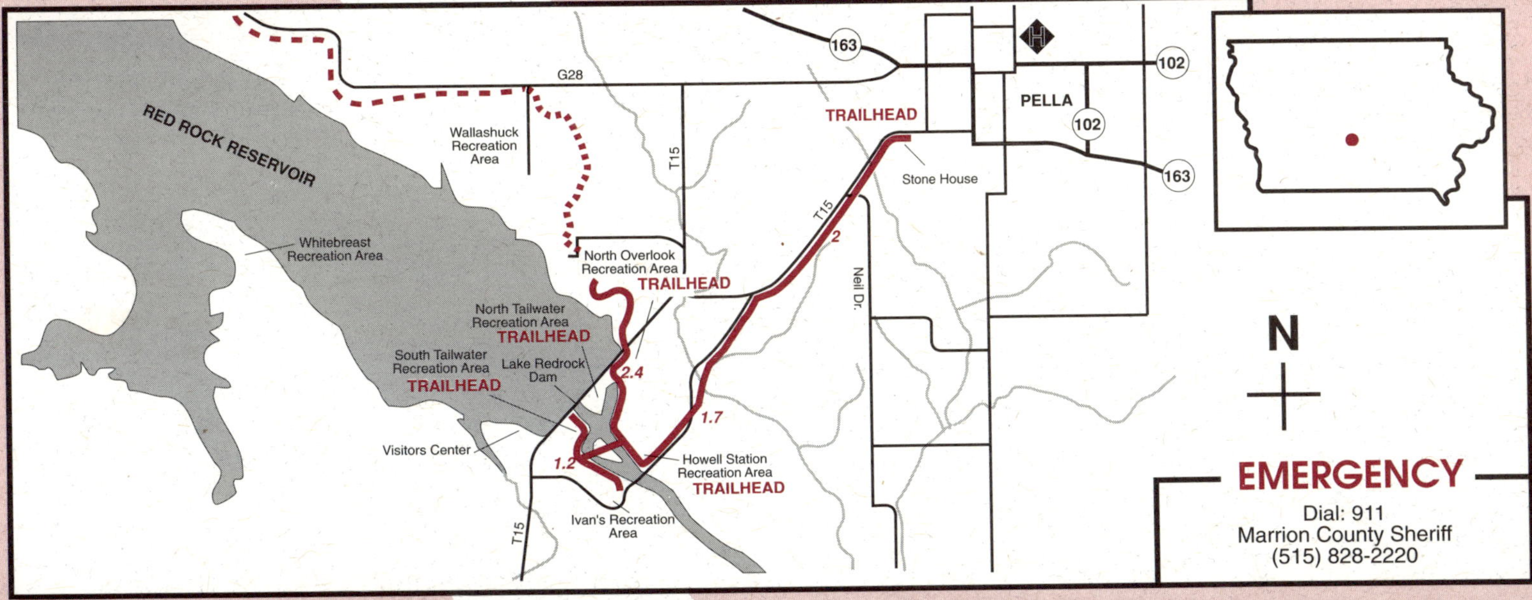

EMERGENCY
Dial: 911
Marion County Sheriff
(515) 828-2220

Trailheads:
- Howell Station Recreation Area
- Ivan's Recreation Area
- South Tailwater Recreation Area
- North Tailwater Recreation Area
- North Overlook Recreation Area
- Wallashuck Recreation Area
- Whitebreast Recreation Area
- Visitors Center
- Lake Red Rock Dam
- Stone House
- Pella

Roads: 163, 102, T15, G28, Neil Dr.

Trail distances: 1.2, 1.7, 2.4, 2

RED ROCK RESERVOIR

VOLKSWEG TRAIL - Marion County

Volksweg is a Dutch word meaning "people's path," and this unique trail serves as a path connecting the picturesque city of Pella to the recreation areas of Lake Red Rock. The section of the trail linking Pella to the lake is parallel to, but separate from, the county road. After reaching Howell Station Campground at Lake Red Rock, the trail follows the Des Moines River and winds through the North Overlook woods. Plans include an additional section leading to Wallashuck Campground to be completed in 1994.

The trail traverses timbered areas, restored prairies, pine plantations and open fields, and offers spectacular views of Lake Red Rock. Visitors can catch glimpses of game and non-game animals and a wide variety of birds. Eagles are frequently seen in the tailwater area. Benches placed along the trail act as scenic rest stops. For those looking for more action, recreational opportunities at the lake include picnic areas, camping, hiking trails, swimming and boating.

Just as the trail is diverse, so are area events. Lake Red Rock hosts Red Rock Bald Eagle Days in February. Pella's Dutch heritage is celebrated during the famous Pella Tulip Time festival that takes place in May. August brings the Knoxville Nationals to the Knoxville Raceway, south of Lake Red Rock.

Tourism information can be obtained from the Pella Chamber of Commerce, 518 Franklin Street, Pella, Iowa 50219, (515) 628-2626; or the U.S. Army Corps of Engineers listed below.

 Some sections of the trail have grades of 5% - 7%, while others are less than 3%. Please call sources listed below for more information.

PELLA
Trailhead at University and Central Drive: parking*
City facilities
Bed & breakfasts
Bicycle shop/repair
City parks
County parks
Golf course
Groceries
Hospital
Hotels/motels
Information center
Restaurants

LAKE RED ROCK
Trailhead at Howell Station Landing off T-15, 2 miles south of Pella: parking*, restrooms*, drinking water, picnic tables, trail maps/information, camping

Trailhead at South Tailwater Recreation Area off T-15 at south end of dam: parking*, restrooms, drinking water, picnic tables, trail maps/information, visitors center

Tralhead at North Tailwater Recreation Area off T-15, 2 miles south of Pella: parking*, restrooms, drinking water, picnic tables, trail maps/information

Trailhead at North Overlook Picnic Area off T-15 at north end of the dam: parking*, restrooms, drinking water, picnic tables, trail maps/information, camping, beach

*Handicap-accessible

HOURS: Open year-round, no restrictive hours. **FEE:** No user fee required.
TRAIL FACTS: Total miles: 16; **Miles completed:** 7.5; **Surfacing:** Asphalt; **Restrictions:** Part of the trail is closed during the deer shotgun season.
INFORMATION: Marion County Conservation Board, Fourth Floor, Courthouse, Knoxville, Iowa 50138; (515) 828-2213 or the U.S. Army Corps of Engineers, Red Rock Dam & Lake Red Rock, R.R. 3, Box 149A, Knoxville, Iowa 50138; (515) 828-7522

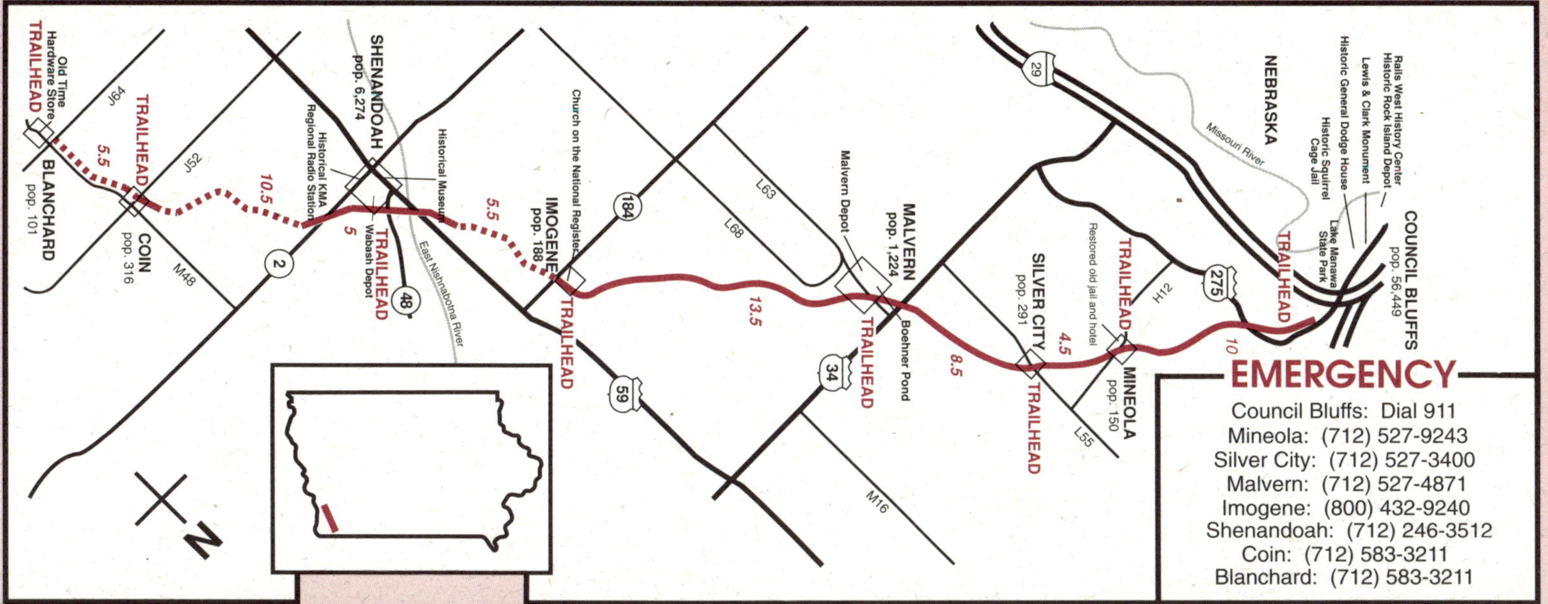

WABASH TRACE NATURE TRAIL 35

EMERGENCY

Council Bluffs: Dial 911
Mineola: (712) 527-9243
Silver City: (712) 527-3400
Malvern: (712) 527-4871
Imogene: (800) 432-9240
Shenandoah: (712) 246-3512
Coin: (712) 583-3211
Blanchard: (712) 583-3211

Trail Segments and Locations

- **COUNCIL BLUFFS** pop. 56,449 — TRAILHEAD
  - Rails West History Center
  - Historic Rock Island Depot
  - Lewis & Clark Monument
  - Historic General Dodge House
  - Historic Squirrel Cage Jail
  - Lake Manawa State Park
  - Missouri River
  - NEBRASKA
  - US 275, I-29
- 10 miles to MINEOLA
- **MINEOLA** pop. 150 — TRAILHEAD
  - L55, H12
- 4.5 miles to SILVER CITY
- **SILVER CITY** pop. 291 — TRAILHEAD
  - Restored old jail and hotel
  - N16
- 8.5 miles to MALVERN
- **MALVERN** pop. 1,224 — TRAILHEAD
  - Boehner Pond
  - Malvern Depot
  - US 34, L63, L68
- 13.5 miles to IMOGENE
- **IMOGENE** pop. 188 — TRAILHEAD
  - Church on the National Register
  - US 59, 184
  - East Nishnabotna River
- 5.5 miles to SHENANDOAH
- **SHENANDOAH** pop. 6,274
  - Historical Museum
  - Historical KMA Regional Radio Station
  - Wabash Depot — TRAILHEAD
  - US 48, 2
- 5 miles / 10.5 miles to COIN
- **COIN** pop. 316 — TRAILHEAD
  - M48, J55
- 5.5 miles to BLANCHARD
- **BLANCHARD** pop. 101 — TRAILHEAD
  - Old Time Hardware Store
  - J64

WABASH TRACE NATURE TRAIL - Page, Fremont, Mills and Pottawattamie Counties

This 63-mile trail is a sanctuary filled with natural wonders. On the trail heading south from Council Bluffs, travel through the picturesque loess hills, a geological formation only found to this great extent here and in China. Observant travelers will see an abundance of wildlife. The trail is also a botanical wonder, alive with trees that form long, colorful tunnels, transforming the trail's appearance each season. Some wild plants on the trail have been identified nowhere else in Iowa, and at the southern end, native prairie species can be found.

The Wabash Trace also holds historical wonders. The Wabash Depot of Shenandoah, listed on the National Register of Historic Places, has been recently restored and moved to Sportsman Park. The Malvern Depot was restored as an Eagle Scout project.

This trail is scheduled for completion in 1995. For tourist information, contact Council Bluffs Convention & Visitors Bureau, 119 S. Main, Council Bluffs, Iowa 51501, (712) 325-1000; or Shenandoah Chamber of Commerce, 403 W. Sheridan, Shenadoah, Iowa 51601, (712) 246-3260.

COUNCIL BLUFFS
Trailhead south of Lewis Central School off Hwy. 275, near I-29: parking*, restrooms*
City facilities
Bed & breakfast
Bike shop/repair
Camping
Groceries
Hospitals
Lodging
Picnicking
Restaurants
Trail passes

MINEOLA
Trailhead at north end of Mineola: parking*, picnic tables
City facilities
Restaurant
Trail passes

SILVER CITY
Trailhead at City Park: parking, picnic tables
City facilities
Convenience store
Restaurant
Trail passes

MALVERN
Trailhead at Main Street: parking*
City facilities
Camping
Convenience store
Grocery
Picnic tables
Restaurants
Trail passes

IMOGENE
Trailhead next to Main Street: parking, picnic tables
City facilities
Restaurant

SHENANDOAH
Trailhead at Sportsman Park on Ferguson Avenue: parking*, restrooms*, picnic tables, drinking water.
Trailhead at Argus Road near cemetery: parking*
City facilities
Bike shop/repair
Camping
Groceries
Hospital
Lodging
Trail passes

COIN
Trailhead at Main Street: parking
City facilities
Bed & breakfast
Camping
Picnic tables

BLANCHARD
Trailhead at Main Street: parking

*Handicap-accessible

HOURS: Open year-round, no restrictive hours. **FEE:** User fee required: $1.00/day or $6.00/year.
TRAIL FACTS: Total miles: 63; **Completed miles:** 42 (Council Bluffs to Imogene: 36.5 miles; Shenandoah: 5 miles; Coin: .5 miles);
Surfacing: Crushed limestone; **Restrictions:** Equestrian use is permitted on a parallel trail on the northern five miles only.
INFORMATION: Bill Hillman at (712) 246-4444

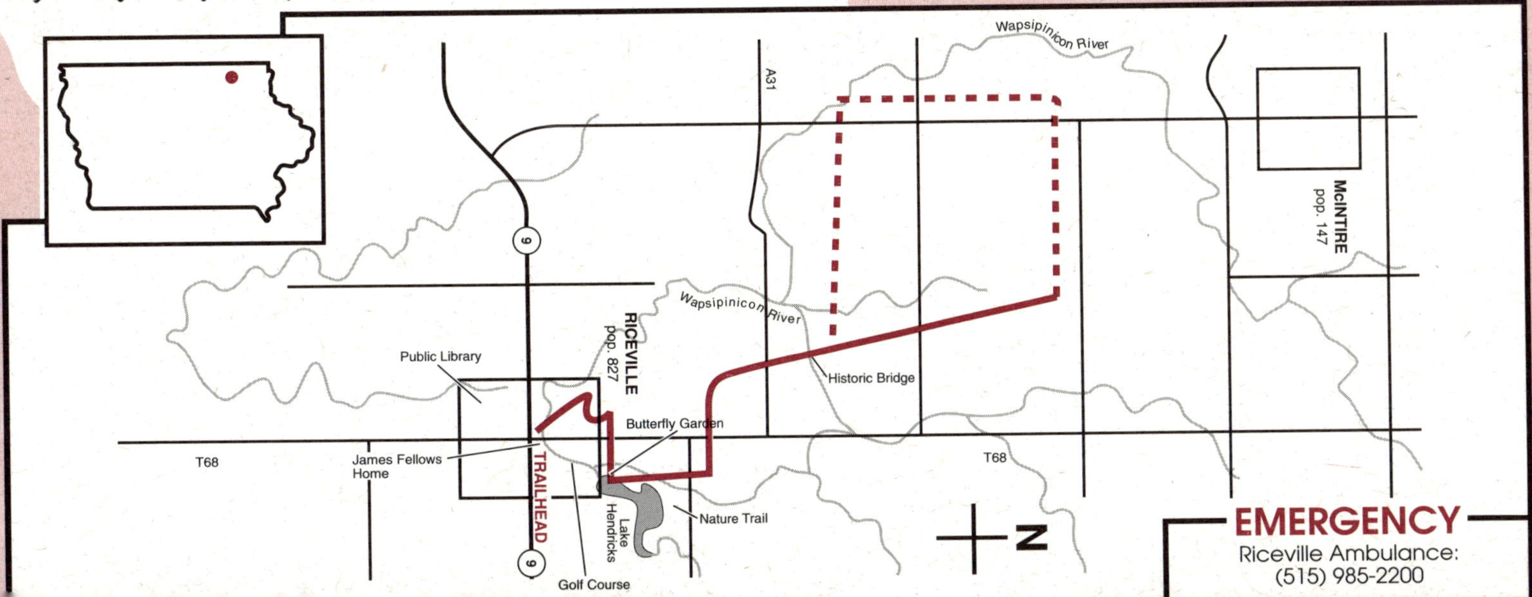

WAPSI-GREAT WESTERN LINE

36

EMERGENCY
Riceville Ambulance:
(515) 985-2200

N

TRAILHEAD

Golf Course
Lake Hendricks
Nature Trail
Butterfly Garden
James Fellows Home
Public Library
RICEVILLE pop. 827
Historic Bridge
Wapsipinicon River
McINTIRE pop. 147
Wapsipinicon River

T68
A31
9

WAPSI-GREAT WESTERN LINE - Howard and Mitchell Counties

The Wapsi-Great Western Line offers segments that run both on the Wapsipinicon River corridor and the abandoned railbed of the Great Western Railroad: it combines the features of both for the ideal trail experience. The 3.5-mile trail starts in Riceville and extends north, traversing hilltops and wide rolling landscape, native prairie and timbered areas. Visitors can see a butterfly garden built into a hillside along the trail and stop at nearby Lake Hendricks for a stroll on the two-mile grass walking path. A future addition will extend the trail to 10 miles by adding a large loop at the north end.

Historical highlights found on the trail include the Little Cedar River Bridge three miles north of the trailhead. Built in 1887, the "Pratt through truss" bridge is one of the few remaining wrought iron truss bridges. Located near the trailhead is the James Fellows Home, listed in the National Register of Historic Places. The Riceville Public Library contains historic opera curtain paintings.

Additional natural attractions can be found in the Riceville area. Hayden Prairie, northeast of Riceville, is the largest blacksoil prairie in Iowa. Sleeping Duck Marsh offers trails for nature study.

Annual trail events include summer and winter outings. June brings the annual Golf Cart Tour, which gives the elderly and persons with handicaps a chance to experience the trail. In late December cross-country skiers can participate in the Christmas Ski. Riceville festivals include Ag Day held in June and the Wapsipinicon Festival and Volksmarch in August.

For tourism information, contact the Mitchell County Conservation Board, 415 Lime Kiln Road, Osage, Iowa 50461; (515) 732-5204.

RICEVILLE
Trailhead on north side of Highway 9: parking*, drinking water
City facilities
Bicycle repair
Camping
City park
County park
Golf course
Groceries
Public showers
Restaurants

LAKE HENDRICKS
Camping
Fishing
Nature trail
Parking
Picnic tables
Restrooms*
 (in summer)
Showers
 (in summer)
Swimming

*Handicap-accessible

HOURS: Open year-round, from 1 hour prior to sunrise to 1 hour after sunset.
FEE: No user fee required.
TRAIL FACTS: Total miles: 10.5; **Miles completed:** 3.5; **Surfacing:** Crushed limestone
INFORMATION: Wapsi-Great Western Line, P.O. Box 116, Riceville, Iowa 50466; (515) 985-4030

NOTES

SPECIAL INFORMATION:

NOTES NOTES NOTES NOTES NOTES NOTES NOTES

Thanks for promoting Iowa trails!

ENJOY IOWA'S RECREATION TRAILS

NEED A COPY OF THIS GUIDE FOR A FRIEND?

Trail guides make great gifts, too! To order additional copies of *Enjoy Iowa's Recreation Trails*, send us the following:

- the number of copies you would like to purchase
- the name, address, city, state and zip of the location where you would like the guides to be mailed
- $6.00 (includes sales tax), plus $1.50 for shipping and handling ($7.50 total) for each trail guide ordered.

Mail your order to:
Iowa Natural Heritage Foundation
505 Fifth Avenue, Suite 444
Des Moines, Iowa 50309-2321

Questions? Call (515) 288-1846.

Supplies are limited. Allow one to two weeks for delivery.